City of Light

Christine Ottaway

ISBN-13: 9798870509891

Cover design by Jason Carter.
http://www.jwccreative.com/

The chasm, the cross, redemption or eternal doom.
The choice is yours.

City of Light

CONTENTS

1   BEGINNING

With a satisfying bang, Jed kicked his bedroom door shut as his mother stormed out of the room. She scooped up his little sister Isla, who was standing on the landing wailing at the noise. It had been the usual argument.

'Have you done your homework?' His mother had grabbed his arm, and tried to pull him away from the PlayStation screen.

'Nah.' Jed had shaken his arm loose, and turned back to the screen.

'Jed. You cannot go on like this.'

'Can't I?' he had smirked at the screen, not even bothering to look at his mother.

'Jed!' His mother's voice rose to an irritated wail of frustration. 'You could do so well.' She inhaled loudly. 'If only you'd try.'

'No point is there?'

'Why not? I don't understand.'

There was no answer, only a yell of triumph from Jed as he leapt up from his chair. 'Got ya. I am victorious.' He punched the air.

He turned to his mother. 'Leave it will you.'

It was at this moment that she flew out of the room.

Jed picked up his phone, and messaged his latest mate Tobi, who headed up the most infamous gang in the school. They had welcomed Jed, who turned to them after the latest bout of trouble in the classroom, due over his completely uncooperative behaviour. Tobi had helped him with a rapidly developing drug habit, and made sure he was constantly in trouble with staff and classmates. All his old school friends had long since abandoned him.

'How zit, bruv?'

Jed used a rude word. 'Another row with my mum. Never let's up.'

'Come roll with us. We're going up the town later.'

'Thanks, but I'm tired.'

'Okay. Your call.'

Jed checked all his social media, undressed and jumped into bed, and after he turned the light off, quickly fell asleep. In the next room, his mother's quiet sobs did not disturb him at all.

Next morning at work, his mother received the phone call she had been dreading.

'Mrs Dawes. This is Mrs Stevens, the school secretary. Jed's head of year has asked if you would come and meet with herself and the headteacher.'

Jed's mother sighed. 'What's he done this time?' Her voice shook a little.

'I'm not sure. I expect they will explain when you come in – again.' There was a definite hint of contempt in the secretary's voice.

Later that day, Jed's mother arrived at the school to be treated to a pitying look from Mrs Stevens. 'Take a seat, Mrs Dawes. Mr Green won't be long now.'

Jed's mother fiddled with her handbag strap and tapped her foot impatiently. At that moment Miss Price, Jed's head of year, arrived. 'Good afternoon, Mrs Dawes.' They shook hands, and she showed them into the headteacher's office.

'I'm sorry to say Mrs Dawes that Jed's behaviour has not improved,' Mr Green said. 'I've frequently spoken to him, but he seems completely disinterested in school or the work. He's rude, disruptive, and makes no attempt to do anything.'

'We've offered all manner of resources to assist him,' Miss Price said. 'He's a bright boy, but he doesn't want to co-operate. He will not be helped.'

'I'm sorry.' Jed's mother took a tissue from her bag and wiped her eyes. 'I don't know what to do. When his dad walked out, he gave up. It's like he stopped living.'

'I am so sorry, Mrs Dawes.' Miss Price's voice was quiet and sympathetic. 'I'm afraid we are concerned that Jed will soon be in trouble with the police. He's taken up with a group of boys who are already sailing pretty close to the wind.'

Jed's mother closed her eyes as more tears leaked from under her eyelids. She shook her head. 'What can I do?'

'We can recommend counselling, but please try to talk to him.'

'He won't listen. He won't talk.'

'Grandparents?'

'No. I'm afraid that's part of the problem. His granddad's death. He won't talk to anyone.'

'We will see what we can arrange, but it won't be soon. There's a long waiting list,' Miss Price said.

Mr Green coughed gently. 'I'm sorry, but in the meantime we do need to give Jed another and final, fixed term suspension of three days. We cannot ignore his behaviour.'

Jed's mother, her face white, stood up. 'I don't know what to say.'

At that moment the bell for the end of the day rang.

'I'll fetch him now.' Jed's mother stumbled out of the door past the disdainful face of Mrs Stevens, and out to the school gate.

In the car on the way to collect Isla from her nursery, Jed's mother told Jed the latest news.

'Good,' Jed said, slumped in his seat. 'Waste of time my going to the dump.'

Jed's mother suddenly braked sharply and pulled to the side of the road. 'Are you going to waste the rest of your life because you father walked out?' she screamed at him. 'It affected me as well, you know. He was my husband. Just as well I haven't given up. You are so selfish, and such a brat. I know you're upset about Granddad, but we can't bring him back. You must move on.' The tirade went on for quite a while as Jed's mother vented all her frustration on him.

Jed slunk lower and lower in the seat, and eventually put his hands over his ears. He turned away to look out of the car window so his mother wouldn't see his eyes brimming with tears. His beloved granddad had helped Jed to pick up the pieces of his life and cope. It had been the greatest act of betrayal therefore, when his grandfather had suddenly died only three months after his father had walked out. His heart had shattered, and he knew he would never get over it.

Finally, his mother ran out of steam. Without another word, she started the car, and in silence they collected Isla, and drove home.

For three days Jed had the house to himself, and though he spent hours on the computer, and every night slunk out the door to hang out in town with Tobi, his mother's words rattled round and round in his head.

2 THE ACCIDENT

On the Monday following his suspension, Jed sauntered out to his mum's car. His breath hung white in the frosty air as he slammed the front door shut, and shivered.

'Jed. Please hurry up. We're late.' His mother and Isla were in the car, seat belts fastened.

Jed shrugged, opened the front car door, and slumped into the seat. Jed's mother jammed her foot on the accelerator, as the car shot backwards out of the driveway, only just missing a car slithering up the icy street. The back wheels spun before gaining a grip, narrowly missing a parked vehicle, and with an exasperated breath Jed's mother sped up towards the main road.

Jed's mother pushed the vehicle out into a line of traffic, causing a lorry to hoot so loudly that even Jed looked up. They made slow progress.

'We are all going to be so late, Jed, thanks to you.' His mum glared at him. Jed pulled his hood down lower, as he sank deeper in the seat, as if trying to disappear.

A gap opened up in the traffic, and Jed's mother sped into the outside lane to try to gain a few metres. The car hit a patch of black ice and started to spin out of control. Jed sat up, pushed back his hood as the car slid with nothing to hinder its progress towards a massive lorry.

'Mum!' Jed's scream pierced the car.

'I can't stop,' his mother shouted, her hands wrestling the steering wheel to no effect.

'Mummy!' Isla sobbed from her car seat in the back.

In what seemed like slow motion, Jed felt the back of the car skidding, spinning nearer and nearer to the lorry. He glanced at the appalled face of the lorry driver who was trying to stop, turn, do anything to avoid the collision, but in the heavy morning traffic, he was out of options.

With the horrendous sound of metal careering into metal, followed by shattering glass, and his mother's shrill cry of terror, their car smashed into the lorry. For a moment, Jed felt excruciating agony as his arm crunched into the car door, bent by the impact, and a terrible pain ripped into his abdomen. The silence was deafening. A bitter taste filled Jed's mouth, and he smelt petrol as he lost consciousness.

He didn't see the man running towards their car tossing a cigarette butt on the road. He certainly wasn't aware of the explosion that engulfed the car in flames, as a spark from the cigarette butt ignited the leaking petrol. He didn't see the man whose careless action caused the blast, try to stamp out the flames. He didn't hear his sister's sobs, or the screams from the frightened passers-by, who watched in horror as a young man yanked open his mother's door, and dragged her from the blaze.

He never felt the heat from the flames that singed his nostrils and burnt his clothes. He never saw the man whose hands were badly burnt as he hauled the back door of the car open and somehow released his little sister from her car seat. He never knew that men were trying to prise open his car door using fists, feet, and even a crowbar, but it was too dented and too close to the lorry to free him from the burning wreck.

He felt, saw, heard, smelt, and tasted nothing as he slipped into blackness.

3 ERM

Everything was still black as Jed prised his eyes open. His left arm was in agony, and he took his left wrist in his right hand to try to support it. The pain in his arm eased slightly, but his right hand felt tender and sore, and agonising tingles ran up his arm.

He checked his body. Head – aching and was that blood he could feel on his cheek? Dreadful pain in his stomach like someone was stabbing him with a blunt knife. Back – sore. Legs? He moved first his left – ouch and then his right – okay. He was trying to work out how to sit up when he heard a voice, with a heavy East London accent.

'New arrival.'

At that moment, subdued lighting bathed the place in a dim glow that gradually increased until Jed could take in his surroundings. He was lying in a cubicle surrounded by curtains, and two burly medics dressed not in scrubs, but in smart white uniforms trimmed with navy.

'Hello. Glad to see you're awake. We'll have you

sorted out in no time, and on your way.'

'I wasn't too hurt in the crash, then?' Jed looked into the medic's rather battered face, which resembled a retired boxer's, with red cheeks and a broken nose, but his eyes twinkled, and Jed felt comforted.

'Oh. I wouldn't say that, but we can fix most things.'

The other medic who was taller, much thinner, but muscular with ginger hair and matching goatee beard and moustache smiled at Jed as he started to cut his clothes away. Jed yelled in pain as lumps of flesh seemed to be ripped off with his clothes, and a cloth was placed over his lower body.

Jed's eyes flicked from left to right, hoping someone might give him something for the pain. 'Where am I?' His voice sounded croaky.

'Nurse. Water.'

The curtains were pushed aside, and a large nurse who looked ready to compete in Pro Wrestling marched in with a water bottle and sprayed a jet of warm water through his half-open lips to soothe his swollen tongue, and ease away the dryness. He coughed making as little movement as possible, but winced at the sharp pain in his chest that ran down into his belly.

'Reg. Check out the chest,' the first medic said.

'Yes, boss.'

Reg ran experienced hands over Jed's chest, and when he yelped as Reg touched one sore place, a sharp point pierced his right side just below his armpit.

'That should do it.'

'Check out the abdomen,' the boss said.

He felt pressure on his lower abdomen and groaned as pain exploded round his belly. 'Ruptured spleen.'

Jed wanted to look to see what was happening as he felt an agonising stab in his abdomen, followed by a soothing sensation.

'All good,' Reg said.

Tears had started to drip down Jed's face. The boss doctor smiled at him. 'You're doing well.'

'Now look at the head wound please, Reg.'

'Not bad.'

Jed felt Reg lightly soothe a little cream into the side of his head. The throbbing eased. More water squirted into his mouth.

'Hands are burnt. Nasty burn on his left cheek.'

Reg applied more salve was to his hands and face.

'Nearly there, young fella. Only your broken arm to deal with. Dislocated shoulder.' He looked at the robust nurse. 'Give us a hand, Mavis.'

The boss tucked Jed's left arm under his arm and took hold of his shoulder. Mavis grabbed Jed's wrist to hold him still. Jed felt another sharp pain in his shoulder, which intensified as they applied greater pressure, and he screamed in agony as with a sickening click his shoulder and arm were realigned.

Jed felt more balm applied to his upper left arm and then a dressing wrapped around it. Tears dripped down his cheeks. 'That hurt.'

'All better now.' Mavis massaged his shoulder, and beamed a rather strange smile on the face of such a tough-looking lady.

'Can I go home now?'

'You'll have to walk the Way first.'

'What? Where am I?'

'ERM. We deal with new arrivals. Tend their injuries and get them fit enough for the Way.'

'Way?'

'That's why you're here. Didn't you know? You've arrived to walk the Way.'

'But I was in a car crash. Going to school. Then I was here. Where is here?'

'O yes. That's the other place. You're here now.'

One more squirt of water hit his mouth, and he licked his cracked lips. He was about to ask another question, but was interrupted.

'Try getting up. Carefully now.'

Jed eased himself to a sitting position. He could now see his surrounding more clearly. Blue curtains hung from rails at head height, and surrounding him were trolleys covered in medical instruments, bandages and little tubes of ointment. His three medics watched closely as he started to move.

'Stand up. Slowly.'

Jed leant on his hands to push himself upright. 'Ouch.' Pain shot through his left hand and arm.

'That side will hurt for a bit. Take it easy.'

Mavis dumped a set of clothes on the trolley that he had been lying on. 'Get dressed.'

Taking great care, Jed pulled on underwear, socks and a tracksuit made from a soft, dark material. His hands and left arm were sore, and had light bandages wrapped around them, but the clothes were easy to pull on.

'Reg? Take our young punter to Departures.'

'This way, mate,' Reg said.

Jed started to follow him, but turned back to the others. 'Thanks.'

The boss lifted his hand in acknowledgement, and Mavis smiled, and made a shooing motion. 'Off you go.'

'But where do I go? What do I do?'

'No more questions. You'll find out what you need to know as you need to know it. We all do.'

Jed took a deep breath of frustration, but he was still too sore to argue any more. He turned and followed Reg, out into an area of several cubicles, and from there to the main concourse with a door to the outside. On the right-hand side, above a desk manned by a pretty young lady also dressed in the white uniform, but with red trim a sign said 'Admissions.' Over the desk on the left side, the sign said 'Departures'.

Reg led him to this desk, and winked at an attractive brunette, her frothy curls pinned under her cap, but tendrils of soft hair still strayed around her neck and face. She was dressed in the white uniform which showed off her slim figure beautifully. 'Morning, Jeanette. This one's ready to go.'

'Thank you, Reg,' Jeanette said, and fluttered her long lashes at Reg whose cheeks glowed red.

'Now, young sir.' Jeanette turned her attention to Jed. 'You're obviously ready for the Way after the excellent attention you received from the treatment room.' She flashed a smile at Reg that made his face go an even deeper shade of red. 'Reg?'

'What? Oh yes.' He turned to Jed and handed him a tube of ointment, and a pack of what looked like dressings. 'Use this ointment on your wounds if they are painful especially that arm. Don't put too much pressure on it for a week or so. Use the dressings to keep the wounds clean.'

'A week? I'll give it to my mum. She's good at remembering.' Jed said. 'If you give me my phone or let me borrow one, I'll ring my mum or someone, and they can come and collect me.'

Reg and Jeanette exchanged a look.

'What?' Jed looked around then back at them.

Jeanette smiled in a sympathetic manner. 'Everyone says something like that. No phones here. You have to walk the Way.'

'But aren't I going home?' His voice had a definite panicky squeak to it.

'Of course, but you have to walk the Way to get there.

Depends too on which destination you choose.' She looked at him in the same manner he looked at Ben, a boy in his class with special needs.

'What do you mean?'

Jeanette ignored the question, and reached below the desk, and started placing items on the top. 'Backpack. Water bottle. Fill it over there.' She pointed to a tap on the wall. 'Way manual and compass.' She plonked a book and a small box on the table. 'Tent, cooking utensils and spare set of clothes, and rations for the first few days are already inside.'

Jed looked at her, at Reg and the supplies. 'I don't get it. Where am I going?'

'Once you have gathered all these supplies, out the door over there.' Jeanette pointed.

'But …' Jed looked at their faces, which smiled back at him. 'I want to go home.' His voice rose to a shout. 'Now.'

'You - can - only - reach - home - by - walking - the - Way,' Jeanette said again enunciating each word whilst staring him in the face.

'But …' Glaring at the two of them, he picked up the backpack and stuffed all the other items inside. He stalked over to the tap and filled the water bottle and shoved it into an external pocket. Then, with another angry scowl at Jeanette and Reg who were giggling together, he stomped out towards the door.

'Don't forget your coat and boots,' Reg called.

Jed glanced at his feet, covered in thick socks, but no shoes. Reg pointed to a shoe rack filled with all manner of shoes and boots neatly arranged in size order. With an exasperated sigh, Jed examined the ones that seemed about his size, and tried a few on. He chose a pair of hiking boots that were very comfortable. On the wall nearby, hung spare socks and laces neatly arranged, and he grabbed some, and thrust them into his backpack.

Hanging on hangers were a variety of coats. Jed inspected them and chose the coolest looking one in his size.

'Don't forget. Always home,' Reg said, glancing briefly at him.

Jed scowled at Jeanette and Reg, who gazed deeply into each other's eyes, then stomped to the door, which opened automatically in front of him.

4 THE WAY

The darkness of night was lightening to day as Jed stepped outside. To his right a huge orange sun peered over the horizon.

He was standing outside the modern door of the ERM, which seemed to be set in a cave mouth high up a mountain. Before him, the land sloped away, and in the distance he could see the sea stretching away into the distance. Breakers curled along the shoreline, running and tumbling in white froth until they dissolved upon the beach. To his right the mountain range strode away till the peaks disappeared into low-level cloud.

The day grew lighter and lighter as the orange sun rose in the sky.

To his left Jed saw that the mountain on which he stood was the last in the range. From here the land dropped away in hills and slopes towards the sea, and towards the rest of the country, or wherever he was. In the far distance across valleys, and what looked like farmland, the countryside rose again and hazy, blue peaks filled the far horizon. A strange incandescent glow seeped over those mountains.

There was only one path before him, but it went both left and right. Jed checked both ways, but neither looked better than the other, and there was no signpost.

'Which path? All I want to do is go home? Which way is that?' He curled up his nose and frowned in frustration.

He turned to retrace his steps back into the hospital to ask for clarification, but the door that he had come through had disappeared. All that was in front of him was a rock face. 'What?' He kicked the hard surface.

He glared at the giant sun rising in the sky. 'Not that way.' He turned away. 'I'll try this direction first.'

'Wise choice.' A man wearing a three-piece suit, white shirt and red striped tie and black, highly polished shoes stood up from behind a nearby rock where he appeared to have been waiting. He looked dressed for a day in the City, and his refined accent confirmed this.

'What?' Jed looked at the man hopefully. 'Are you here to help? How do I get home?'

'You have to walk the Way.'

'But where is it, and where am I?'

'Ah.' The man smiled at Jed in a sympathetic manner. 'Not mine to tell, I'm afraid. I can advise you on direction, though.'

'Which way do I go?'

'I couldn't possibly advise a definite direction, but I can guide you when you have chosen.'

'I have no idea where I am, why I'm here, and what I'm supposed to do,' Jed said, his face set in angry lines.

'Ah. The enigma of existence. Philosophers would probably argue that all of us are walking the unknown path of life.' The man sighed, his voice sounding more pompous with every pronouncement.

'You're no flipping help.'

'Am I supposed to be?'

'I thought that was what you were here for.'

'Another disappointment.' The man shrugged with an apologetic look and held his hands out.

'I'm going this way,' Jed said turning along the path that wound down the mountainside towards the sea.

'I can show you some fascinating scenarios should you be interested.' The man said in a soothing voice, as he caught up with Jed who was striding down the road.

'Gaming? Drugs? Drink? What would you like to try?

We can offer all these and many more.' The man turned his head, his blue eyes staring at Jed.

'Gaming?' Jed's voice had an edge of expectancy. 'Depends which ones.'

'We can offer all usual games and a few I am sure you have not played, but which you would love once you have tried them.'

'Maybe.'

His mind flashed back to the endless arguments with his mother about the hours he spent gaming. *It was fun. What's the problem?* He remembered his nastiness to his little sister. She was only four, but when she interrupted his game, he had shoved her hard, and shouted at her. She had run off wailing to their mother, who had come and berated him.

His words rang in his ears. 'What's the matter with everyone round here? Can't I get a game in peace and quiet?'

At that moment, his path joined a much wider track running in both directions.

'Where's this go?' he asked.

'Another outstanding question. Where indeed?' The man said, his voice dripping with false sympathy.

'Well?'

'This is the main path that runs in that direction,' the man held his hand out to the right, 'and that way in the other direction.' He pointed to the left.

'No bloomin' help at all.'

Jed looked around, and then brightened. Away to his right was a building that looked exactly like his school. He checked again. It was indeed the two-storey brick-built building of 1930s architecture, with a row of windows top and bottom, and in the centre a large wooden front door with an ornamental portal over it. Behind, he could see the three-storey building added in the 1960s. He knew that in the distance, newer buildings stretched to the playing fields.

Leaving the man, he marched off to the school. *At last. Maybe a chance to get home.* When he reached the front gate, he walked by habit round the old building to enter by his usual door. Immediately, he saw his classmates by their lockers unpacking their bags, and getting ready for a new day.

He ran up to them. 'Hey Tom! Michael! Ali! I'm back.'

They all ignored him.

'Tom!' He jostled Tom's arm, but his eyes widened in horror when his hand passed right through Tom's arm. He yanked it back, and with great caution waved his hand in front of their faces. Nobody blinked.

'Shame about Jed,' Tom said. 'Bit young to maybe,' his voice dropped, 'die.'

Jed blanched and tried shaking Ali's arm with no response.

'Yeah, but …' Ali looked around. 'He's been a real jerk lately. I mean …. Don't want to speak ill of him but…'

The others nodded and looked at the floor.

A group of girls that Jed had known since his primary school days came up, some with tears in their eyes. 'Heard about Jed?'

'Yeah,' the boys mumbled.

'I was told they're not sure if he will ever come out of the coma,' one girl said, her cheeks wet.

'He used to be great, but since his dad …'

They all looked at one another and grimaced. 'Not nice though.'

'Nah. Wouldn't want that happening to anyone, no matter how gross they'd been.'

Everyone picked up their bags and ambled off, leaving Jed standing there. His mouth was half open in disbelief, and his eyes stared at their retreating backs.

Thought you were my friends. Great pals you've turned out to be.

He punched the lockers, but his fist seemed powerless, only tapping the metal, and his eyes hardened in frustration. He turned, and stomped off out of the building, back the way he had come.

When he reached the path, the man was still there, leaning against a rock, gazing into the distance. 'Not what you expected?'

'Nah.' Jed's face hardened in angry lines.

'Friends are very unreliable.' The man's voice was even more sanctimonious. He reminded Jed of the undertaker they had visited after his granddad's sudden death. He spoke in the same unctuous, insincere way.

'What do you know about it?' Jed scuffed a stone with his boot.

'I am very observant.'

'Yeah, right.'

The man stood up, and walked off down the path, with Jed trailing behind. At that moment, the silky-smooth smell of chocolate filled the air making inhaling an absolute pleasure.

5 THE CHOCOLATE FACTORY

Whoa. Chocolate!' Jed looked around and spotted a metal, pre-fabricated warehouse a little farther along the trail, from which the delicious smell appeared to be wafting. Jed ran past the man and stood before the front window display of the warehouse.

A fountain of gigantic proportions, carved to look like a mountain, was gushing a river of smooth, dark brown chocolate along its slopes, and into a channel designed to resemble a river flowing through the countryside. Along the banks of the chocolate river stood farms and animals created out of all colours of chocolate, decorated with jewel like sweets.

On the slopes of the chocolate mountain, which was covered in white chocolate sprinkles to resemble snow, stood goats, ibex with large horns, and what appeared to be a snow leopard waiting to pounce on an unfortunate ibex.

Jed's eyes were glued to the window trying to take in the entire amazing scene before him.

Farther on, the chocolate river passed through a town, constructed of every imaginable type of confectionary. There were gingerbread houses, schools carved out of a giant cake with intricate icing to depict windows and doors. Behind the school, chocolate figures were playing a soccer match. There was even a zoo with multi-coloured chocolate animals decorated with sweets, icing, and hundreds and thousands.

At that moment, a low, gravelly sort of voice said, 'Care to come inside, guv. Better than just looking at the window display.'

Jed turned to see a bald-headed man, a pair of round spectacles sliding down his nose, dressed in a purple waistcoat over a white shirt, and white gloves standing before him. 'Step this way,' he invited Jed. 'Backpacks over there. Don't want you hitting any of the displays.' Jed dropped his backpack in a cloakroom area manned by a woman similarly dressed in purple and white.

Wide eyed, Jed followed the man inside, and stood gazing upon the most incredible chocolate shop he had ever seen. There were indeed shelves upon shelves of chocolate bars, and bags of sweets, but it was the displays that blew his mind. He wandered around exhibits of Buckingham Palace and the Tower of London all constructed out of chocolate, and exquisitely decorated.

Jed put out his hand to see if it was real and edible, but he received a sharp smack on the hand by the white-gloved man. 'No touching, mate.'

Jed scowled at him.

'Oh gee,' an American voice broke into Jed's marvelling. 'Look at that.'

Jed turned to look at what the voice was admiring. There was a chocolate White House, and what Jed assumed were other significant landmarks of Washington. Jed continued to stare in awe as he meandered round display after display. The Sydney Opera House, the Great Wall of China, the Burj Khalifa literally towered over everything else as it does in Dubai.

'Care to sample the goods, guv?' the man asked.

'Sure, but I don't have any money.'

'Tried the front pocket of your backpack?'

Jed returned to the cloakroom, and rootled in the front pocket, and found some gold coins. Not sure of the currency, though they looked valuable, he took two back to the man.

'That should get you a few items,' the man said. 'Care to start with a drink?'

'Yeah, sounds great.' Jed followed him upstairs to a

bar area, where a variety of pretty girls wearing purple dresses and white aprons were serving all manner of customers. Families sat round tables, elderly shoppers were lingering over chocolate drinks and cakes, and there was a group of teenagers lolling in a corner, sniggering and mucking about with chocolate bars. It soon turned into a noisy chocolate fight with confectionary being used as weapons. A burly member of staff leaned over and broke this up, grabbed the flying sweets, and had a quiet word in the group's ears. They all looked suitably chastened, and calmed down.

One of the waitresses passed Jed a menu. It took a little time to read through all the chocolate options, but in the end Jed chose a hot, white chocolate drink with caramel swirl topped with whipped cream, and decorated with dark chocolate nuggets.

'Great choice, mate,' the man said lightly clapping his hands. 'Give her your money.'

Jed handed the girl one of his coins, and she gave him a few chocolate bars and silver foil wrapped figures as change.

'Bag, sir?' the girl asked, smiling in a vacant way to suggest hers was a boring job.

'Sure.'

The girl handed him a purple paper bag with string

handles, and Jed popped his change into it.

'Sit at one of the tables, and your drink will be with you shortly.'

Jed and his companion sat at a table that overlooked the main shop floor below. Soon, another girl appeared with Jed's drink. It looked amazing. It came in a large glass with a cardboard straw, and Jed admired the thick white liquid with the honey coloured swirls running through it.

'Not sure I'll manage all that,' Jed said. 'That mound of cream is huge.'

'Give it a go.'

'You not having any?'

'Nah. Customers only.' The man shrugged, 'Working here you sort of lose your taste for chocolate.'

Jed grinned and took a sip of the drink. 'Whoa. That's rich.' He took a breath, and another sip. Over the next ten minutes, he consumed all the liquid and ate the dark chocolate sprinkles with a spoon.

'I am so full.' Jed patted his stomach.

'Like to buy some chocolate to eat as you walk?' the man asked.

'I won't need to eat anything for hours now, but it

would be handy if I got peckish later.'

'This way then.' The man led him back downstairs to the shop floor, around the extraordinary displays to the shelves of chocolate bars, foil wrapped chocolate figurines, and even bags of ordinary sweets.

Jed avoided the display of Easter eggs. It brought back unpleasant memories of how badly he had treated his other grandparents. They had brought him and Isla a huge Easter egg each, but Jed handed his back. 'No thanks,' he had said. The look of hurt disappointment on their faces still haunted him.

Instead, Jed selected a large chocolate bar loaded with nuts and fruit, and another one with pieces of biscuits and honeycomb. He turned to the man. 'Funny. I'm feeling hungry already.'

'Really?' The man did not look surprised. 'Want another drink or a chocolate snack?'

'Yeah.' Jed ran ahead, back upstairs to the bar, and grabbed a menu. He had already thought of the snack he fancied; a milk chocolate sandwich made from gingerbread with mint flavoured jam and cream running through it. 'And a glass of water, thanks.'

'Sorry. No water.'

'I'll get the water from my bag.'

'Only drinks allowed are those bought on the

premises. Can offer you milk?'

'Alright.' Jed was feeling slightly nauseous at the thought of the sandwich, but his stomach was grumbling with emptiness.

The sandwich and milk arrived, and Jed nibbled at it. The joy of all this chocolate was passing. *Never thought I'd say it, but I'd love an apple.* He laughed to himself.

The man poked his arm. 'Care to share the joke?'

'Nah. Not funny really.' He pushed the half-eaten sandwich away from him. 'I've used most of my money already. I don't think I'll bother buying any more.'

The man looked shocked. 'But you might get hungry later.'

'This stuff is no good. Even after all that, I'm still hungry.' He glared at the man. 'What's wrong with it?'

'Wrong with it? Best quality chocolate. Let me show you some other things.'

'No thanks. Nothing round here seems to be what it should be.'

'No complaints before.' The man looked offended.

'Yeah. Well, I'm off thanks.' Jed plodded back down the stairs, wove his way around all the magnificent displays, picked up his backpack, and shaking his head went outside.

He turned to look back at the window displays. 'Very disappointing.'

His companion from earlier was waiting for him. 'Didn't turn out as expected?'

'Nah. Looked amazing, even tasted good, but it didn't satisfy.' Jed sighed. 'How do I get home?'

The man ignored his question. 'How about a little gaming to take your mind off your disappointment?'

Jed took a deep breath. 'Lead on.'

6 THE GAMING ROOMS

They walked until in the distance Jed could see flashing neon signs indicating an arcade. As the man led Jed nearer, he joined more and more men and women, also heading that way.

Something stirred in Jed, the deep longing to sit at a screen, and engross himself in a game. He never seemed to tire of any game; the constant thrill of strategizing and getting the better of his opponents never wavered. It energised him.

The man took him into the arcade where a pair of bouncers, men nearly as broad as they were tall, wearing black coats over a dinner jacket, and a black bowtie manned the door. They nodded to the man.

'Okay, fella,' they said to Jed. 'Your bag goes in a locker. No back packs allowed on the premises.' They pointed to the left, where there was a row of lockers. Jed strolled over, and threw his backpack, which he had not even looked inside since he left ERM, into an empty locker. He locked the door, and pocketed the key.

As he wandered back to the foyer, he gazed around. The few slot machines at the front were barely occupied, but further back, Jed saw row upon row of gaming machines with men and women sitting pouring money into the slots, and watching fascinated as the symbols and numbers rolled. When the screen finished, their shoulders slumped in disappointment at their loss, before they poured more money into the slot. Every time they ran out of money, they wandered as if drugged, to a desk where a woman, dressed in a smart black frock, her hair and makeup immaculate handed them more tokens after they signed a long sheet.

'Another punter for you, Susie,' the man said as he led Jed to a different lady, wearing the uniform of a white blouse, short black skirt and a little red bow tie. Her face was heavily made up with large lips covered in thick red lipstick.

'Thanks, Magnus. See ya.'

The man turned and strolled out without a backward glance or any farewell.

'What's your game?' The woman's American accent sounded as if it had strayed in from an old television series.

'Not fussy. Like most things but playing *Skybattle* at the moment.'

'How ya doing?'

'Okay.' Jed smirked. 'Better than most of my mates.'

The woman nodded in appreciation. 'See we'll have to set you up with *Planet Invasion*. Takes a bit of getting used to, but very satisfying.'

She led Jed over to a desk and turned a screen around. 'Register here for your logon.'

Jed typed in a new user name, and a password.

'Okay. Give you a thousand units to get you started. Usual things. As you progress, you'll be able to buy better armaments and outfits, and gain greater abilities.'

Jed nodded.

'Over here.' She led Jed to a quiet corner, and left him sitting at a console, and enormous screen. It was already loaded with *Planet Invasion*.

'This is more like it.' Jed settled down and began to play. He quickly acclimatised himself to the game exploring the new worlds, and the creatures that inhabited it. Now and then a pretty girl, with long hair hanging down her back and wearing a black dress and little white apron brought him a drink.

The first time, he looked at her and her tray of drinks. 'There's water in my backpack. I'll get that, thanks.'

'No external drinks allowed.' She smiled at him, and Jed's pulse quickened. 'This one's very good.' She pointed to a deep blue drink that fizzed forming bubbles not only in the drink but also in a haze over the surface.

Jed took a sip and blinked. The bubbles irritated his nose, but it tasted delicious.

'I'll put it on your tab.'

Jed nodded but quickly forgetting the girl, he went back to his game.

He played on and on, not noticing the passing of time. The girl appeared at his side at regular intervals with drinks and sandwiches. After a while, he blinked as his eyes started to lose focus, and his head nodded onto his chest.

'Need a booster?' the girl asked.

'What?' Jed stared blearily at her.

'A booster? Keep you awake?'

'Oh, yeah. Thanks.'

He felt a prick in his upper arm, and soon he started to buzz again. It reminded him of Poppers which he had started to take. Tobi was always happy to supply anything in that line.

A pang of guilt crossed his mind. He'd stolen out of his mother's purse to get his last fix. He quickly squashed the thought, along with the guilt, as he returned to the game. It seemed to have endless levels and endless possibilities. Jed played on.

He had no idea how long he had been there till a girl about his age came up, and bumped hard into him.

'Here. Watch out.' Jed turned on her. 'I lost a droid because of you.'

She shoved him hard again, the whites of her brown eyes blazing out of her dark brown face, that glistened in the light of the screen. The beads on the end of her many plaits jangled to match the irritation on her face.

'What's your trouble? Clear off.' Jed tried to push her away, but his arms had little strength.

'How long have you been here?' She glared at him, shaking his hands loose from the controller that dropped to the floor.

'I dunno. Who cares?'

'You should, for a starter. You're hooked. If you don't get out soon, you'll never make it.'

'What do you care? You're not my mum.' He turned back to the screen, fishing around for the controller.

She pushed him hard off the chair. 'How many of

those drinks have you had?'

Jed went red as he tried to stand up. 'Dunno. Lots, I expect.' He staggered slightly.

'Do you know what's in those drinks?'

Jed shook his head.

'Have they given you one of their boosters?'

'Maybe,' he mumbled. He sat down hard on the chair, his head in his hands.

'How many?'

Jed shrugged. He tried to fish around for the controller, but the girl whipped it away from him.

'We must get you out of here, fast.'

At that moment, the girl appeared carrying her tray of drinks. 'Is there a problem?'

'No, but there will be if he doesn't get out of here soon.' The girl scowled at her.

'He can't leave without settling his bill.' The girl tried to block their path.

'How much do you owe?' The new girl's eyes pierced into Jed's befuddled brain. He shrugged.

'Honestly. You're more of a plonker than I thought.'

She grabbed Jed by the arm, and pushed the waitress aside so her tray of drinks fell on the floor. She dragged Jed behind her out towards the exit.

'You can't leave without settling your account.' The girl's voice floated after them.

They pushed past the gamers sitting at the slot machines, out towards the entrance. The two bouncers guarding the door blocked their path. 'He can't leave here.'

'Why not?' The girl's eyes were furious as she tried to barge past them.

'Outstanding account.'

'Money by false pretences. Drugging a minor and letting an underage person drink your spiked cocktails.' She scowled at them. 'Get out of the way.'

The bouncers shuffled but would not budge.

'I said. Get out of the way.' The girl shoved the bouncers aside, dragging Jed behind her by the front of his coat, into the fresh air of night.

She walked over to a bush and picked up a backpack hidden underneath it.

Jed had collapsed on the ground only a few metres from the entrance. 'My backpack,' he mumbled as he started to vomit.

The girl grabbed him by the arm and hauled him away on his knees until he was behind the bushes. 'Key?' She held out her hand, and Jed fumbled in his pocket, and gave her the key. 'Stay here.'

She disappeared, and Jed lay on the ground groaning and vomiting. She shortly re-appeared carrying his backpack, and dropped it beside him.

'My head's killing me,' Jed said, almost crying.

'I'm not surprised after all that rubbish they've shovelled into you. Got any painkillers in your backpack?'

'Maybe.' He tried to open it, but fumbled the zips, and quickly gave up, flopping down again on the ground, groaning. The girl wrenched open the pack and searched inside.

'Have you looked in here or used any of the things you were given?' Her eyes were angry.

'No. Go away. I feel rubbish.'

'You'll feel even worse if you don't take these.' She handed him some pills and his bottle of water. 'I don't know why I bother.'

'Neither do I,' Jed said in a whining voice, looking very sorry for himself. 'You should have left me.'

'You do know you would have become a mindless

zombie or something worse, if I hadn't dragged you out.' She pulled his arm. 'Come on. Get on your feet. I've pitched my tent near here. You can try sleeping it off.'

Jed staggered upright and followed the girl down the track. 'What's your name?'

'Melanie.'

Jed staggered behind her down the path. 'Won't those blokes want their money?'

'They might, but there're loads of idiots like you, so I doubt if they need to.'

Jed collapsed again.

'Fortunately, it's more trouble than it's worth for them to try to recover what you owe.'

'Thanks, Mel.'

'Melanie. Don't like Mel.'

'Melanie.' Jed curled up to make himself as comfortable as possible on the edge of the path.

'Oh no you don't.' Melanie pulled on his arm.

Jed groaned. 'Leave me alone.'

'I do that, and you'll be lying here in the morning with no clothes and no backpack.'

'What?' Jed gazed at her bleary-eyed, before his head fell back on his arms.

'Thieves. Take anything and everything.'

'Where's your tent?' He mumbled into his arms.

'With others. Safety in numbers.' She kicked his back. 'Now stand up.'

Moaning, Jed raised himself onto his hands and knees, before collapsing again. His left arm ached from the road accident.

'Get up!' Melanie shouted, and leant over and shoved him so hard he rolled into a bush.

'Stop it.' Jed rolled out of the bush and onto all fours again. 'I'm coming.' He staggered onto his feet. 'Alright. Let's go.' He tried to pick up his backpack, but that almost caused him to fall over again.

'Give it here.' Melanie hitched his backpack onto her back and placed her backpack on her front. She gripped Jed's left arm. 'Move!'

'Ow. Not that arm.'

Melanie shook her head and grabbed his other arm.

It took about half an hour with stops for Jed to vomit, and then drink more water, before they turned off the path. Each time Jed felt a little better than before. It was dark, and when they reach the campsite, all was quiet.

'Here's my tent,' Melanie said after picking her way between tents of all sizes, lighting the way with a torch. She dropped the backpacks on the ground by the door of the tent. 'There're latrines and water over there.' She pointed to the edge of the encampment. 'Keep it quiet. Everyone's asleep.'

After using the latrines, Jed fell into Melanie's tent. She had laid out his sleeping bag, which she must have retrieved from his backpack.

Jed took off his boots and his outer coat, both of which were spattered with vomit, and crawled into his sleeping bag, and fell fast asleep.

All night violent dreams troubled his sleep. He muttered and tossed and turned. Jed was unaware of Melanie wiping his head with a cool cloth until he settled back to sleep. Each time she woke and helped him, she whispered to someone in the darkness.

Even when the camp started to stir next morning, and people were chatting to their neighbours as they ate breakfast, and prepared for their day, Jed and Melanie slept on. By the time the huge orange sun was high in the sky, most people had left, and eventually by the middle of the morning, Melanie awoke.

She went and fetched water, and boiled some on a

little portable stove she dug out of her backpack. She made hot drinks and took one to Jed who was stirring.

'Thanks.' Jed smiled at her. 'What time is it?'

'Late morning. How are you feeling?'

Jed nodded. 'Better, thanks.' He shuddered. 'I felt really rough last night.'

'I noticed. How did you sleep?'

'Good.' Jed wrinkled his nose. 'Horrible dreams, though.'

'Not surprising with all that rubbish inside you.'

Jed looked at Melanie properly for the first time. Her dark skin glowed, and her brown eyes sparkled with life. Her hair was plaited into a dozen plaits that ran from forehead to the nape of her neck. She was quite short, but what she lacked in stature was more than made up by her determined presence.

'Why did you come and get me? How did you know?'

'Yeshua told me to find you.'

'Who?'

'Yeshua.'

Jed shrugged. 'Don't know who you're talking about.'

'You will.' Melanie sipped her drink. 'We'll stay here today to give you time to recover properly.'

'Then what?' Jed drained his mug.

'Back to the Way.'

Jed shook his head slowly. 'No idea what you're talking about. All I want is to go home.'

Melanie pulled an exasperated face. 'That's what we're all here for. To walk the Way and get home.'

For a moment Jed's eyes brightened, but then he yawned twice so wide his teeth almost fell out. 'Can I go back to sleep?'

'Really! Have something to eat first.' She pointed to his backpack. 'You should have a Wayfarer bar. They're high energy.'

Jed opened his backpack and rootled inside. 'This?' he held up a bar, slightly larger than a chocolate bar, and wrapped in purple, silver foil.

'That's it.' Melanie was eating a sandwich.

Jed peeled back the wrapper and stared at the bar. 'Is this like one of those chocolate bars?'

'Nothing like.'

He took a small nibble. 'Hmm, cool. What's in it?' He took a larger bite and then another. 'Funny. It's not getting any smaller.'

'Yeah. Wayfarer bars are like that,' Melanie said. 'They last as long as you need them. Don't know how it works.'

'Great. How many do I have I?' He looked inside his bag.

'There's only ever one,' Melanie said. 'They'll be one if you need it.'

'Weird.' Jed took a last bite. 'I'm full. Will it last?'

'Yup. Fills you up properly.' Melanie sat back and pulled out a book. 'This is a Way manual; we all have one. You need to start reading this. It'll help stop you from falling into places like the gaming rooms.'

'It was that bloke in a suit that suggested it,' Jed said, glaring around as if the man might be nearby.

'Magnus?' Melanie laughed. 'He's always trying to get idiots into places they shouldn't go.'

'Thanks.' Jed scowled at her. 'How was I supposed to know?'

'If it sounds too good to be true, it is,' Melanie said. 'You know obsessive gaming is rubbish, didn't you?'

'I like it. Hasn't harmed me so far.' He blushed as he remembered all the arguments with his mother.

'Mm. You may like to reconsider that. Magnus always tries to tempt people on their weaknesses.'

Jed glared at her. 'I'm going to have a snooze.'

Melanie gave a little wave. 'Sleep well.'

Jed crawled back into the tent, but lay there mulling over what Melanie had said.

Yeshua? The Way? All I want is my bed at home.

7 BACK TO THE WAY

That's better,' Jed said, when he woke a few hours later. 'Think I've slept the worst of it off now.'

Melanie had been lying snoozing in the sun while he slept. 'Great. Why don't you take a shower?' She pointed to a low wooden block that looked like a large garden shed. 'Everyone will start arriving for the night soon. They'll want a shower. Best to get in first.'

'Okay.'

He was just about to collect a towel and wash things, when Jed noticed beside Melanie what looked like a miniature games set. It was a box about half the size of a small cereal carton but square. The box had four quarters in which were a miniature chess pieces, chequers, a tiny solitaire board and a pack of cards.

Separate from the box was a board that folded into quarters, so it was the same size as the box, and lying next to it was a lid that appeared to clip onto the board, securing everything into a neat travelling set.

'That's brilliant,' Jed said, as he picked up a tiny chess piece and fingered it.

'Careful. They're easy to lose.'

Jed examined the chess pieces, each exquisitely made, not of cheap plastic, but carved in wood. It was beautifully crafted.

'Where did you get it?'

'Won it in a raffle.' Melanie's brown eyes sparkled.

'Yeah right.'

Jed ducked into the tent and looked in his backpack for the first time. His water bottle had been in a pocket on the side, and he knew there were coins in the front pocket. He remembered stuffing spare clothes in the pack, but he'd forgotten about the tent and sleeping bag, and one of those lightweight towels that wrap up very small.

He took everything out and laid it on his bed. He found the first aid items the medics had given him, including the pack of pills Melanie had used last night. They had given him two lightweight plates, a bowl, cutlery and even some pots and pans to cook with. Everything was solid but light. He also discovered the Way manual, a box and a beautiful purple embroidered bag, the size of a wash bag, as well as a bag of toiletries. He shoved them all away under the spare clothes to hide them, along with his guilty thoughts.

I didn't know there was all this stuff in there. Nobody told me. He thumped fist into palm. His mother's voice rang in his head. 'You need to grow up Jed and stop expecting everyone else to tell you what to do.'

It's all my dad's fault. He should have been there, and not walked out on us like that. If Granddad hadn't died, he would have helped me.

He picked up his towel, wash bag and a tube of healing ointment that the medics had given him, and glaring at Melanie he stomped off to the showers. Melanie looked after him. 'What's bugging him?'

After his shower, Jed applied some ointment onto his bruises and burns, which were looking better. He then arranged his hair as he usually did to show how cool he was, but it was difficult with no gel or comb, which was in his backpack. Looking at himself in the mirror, he pouted. *I look a right nerd.*

He ambled back to Melanie feeling clean, but still wearing his dirty clothes. 'You might like to wash your clothes and your coat's splattered with sick.'

'Thanks, Mum.' His voice was heavy with sarcasm. 'Where's the washing machine?'

'The sinks are next to the shower block. Here.' She threw him a container with washing powder in. 'Need a hand?' Her eyes were innocent looking.

'No.' Jed crawled into the tent, changed his clothes, scooped the dirty ones and his coat up and tramped off to the find the sinks.

Jed had never hand-washed anything before, so there was a large amount of water and suds slopping around. Eventually, his clothes and coat were clean, but dripping wet.

'Here.' Melanie appeared at his side. 'There's a handy machine to get water out of wet washing.' She showed Jed a round tub into which he stuffed his clothes. As she shut the lid, he heard the tub whirring, and water poured out of a spout at the bottom.

'Why are there no washing machines?'

'There are. Thought you'd like the experience of hand washing.' She laughed.

'Ha. Ha.' Jed scowled at her, and was about to march off when she said, 'Don't forget your clothes.'

'Tumble dryer?'

'Washing line.' She pointed to three or four long lines of rope with pegs dotted along them. Melanie helped Jed hang his clothes on the line, another first for him.

'Come on. We've a lot to talk about.'

They returned to the tent and sat down on the ground outside.

'Jed, we're all walking the Way. Each one of us has to decide where we're going. There's Yeshua's path or there are other ways but only two destinations.'

Jed stared at her, trying to take it all in.

'We've each been given a Way manual and a compass to help us. Where are yours?'

'In there.' Jed pointed into the tent. 'I'll get it.'

He fingered the beautiful purple bag and picked it up and the Way manual and box, and re-joined Melanie.

'The Way manual is essential, not only to get things right day by day, but when you need specific guidance about what to do.'

Jed looked at the unopened book in his hand. 'Who made you such an expert?'

'I'm not an expert. Just been walking the Way longer than you.'

She picked up her compass and indicated Jed should open his box. Inside was a round compass, but instead of having north, south, east and west on it, it indicated only one direction: HOME.

'It works like any usual compass. Hold it up and it will point the Way you have chosen to be HOME.' Her hand covered her compass. 'Try it.'

Jed held his compass, and the needle quivered till it settled on the direction HOME. Melanie's face looked rather sorrowful. 'Not surprising.'

'Tomorrow, we start out following the Way. We'll find a group to walk with. You never walk alone. That's what landed you in so much trouble.'

Jed blushed, but his eyes were hard. 'I didn't know.'

'Well, you do now.'

He looked at the purple bag. 'What's this?'

'Your Bag of Rewards.'

Jed tried to open it, but he couldn't. He looked questioningly at Melanie.

'You can never open it, but it fills up by itself. If you make it to the City of Light, it turns into rewards.'

'What like chocolate bars?'

'More permanent and precious I think.' She smiled at him. 'Look, there's a lot to take in.'

Jed threw the bag down on the ground. 'So where do we sleep each night?'

'We stop at camps like this which are set up for travellers or bunkhouses or other shelters if there's no camp.'

'How do we get food?' Jed's stomach was rumbling.

'We buy it. Fortunately, I have enough food for tonight, and I expect there's still some in your backpack and a bit of money.'

'Yeah. Will it be enough?'

'We'll have to earn money to get more. There's also food to be foraged along the Way.'

'What - work? Picking stuff?'

'Yes. Work.' Melanie's face was a picture. 'Have you ever done anything useful before?'

'What do you mean? I'm not completely useless.'

Melanie held up her hands, palms outwards. 'Okay. Just seems as if your parents have done everything for you.'

'So your mum didn't do stuff for you.'

'Some of us learnt life the hard way. My mum turned me out on the streets from an early age to beg for money to feed her drug habit.'

'What?'

'I couldn't come home till I had enough money.'

'Really?'

'She wanted me to steal. I refused.' She pulled back her sleeve to reveal a series of what looked like cigarette burns. 'After that we compromised on begging. I ended up here because I was caught in a turf war over drugs. I was trying to stop them slash my mum's face, so they stabbed me instead.'

Jed's face was a picture of astonishment.

Melanie's face brightened. 'Best thing that happened to me.'

'What?'

'Met Yeshua and now you Jed.'

Jed shook his head and stared at the ground. All his mother asked him to do was tidy his room, do his homework, help with the washing up. He'd been too selfish or stupid to manage even those simple things. Embarrassed, Jed glared at her. 'How long's this going to take?'

'No idea. We walk until we get home.'

'My house? I mean I am going to find my home, aren't I? That's what I want.' Jed looked up, expectantly.

'Nah. Not that sort of home. But we'll know. Believe me. We'll know.'

8 CHRISTMAS

Jed and Melanie set off from the campsite next morning, walking with a group that seemed to Jed to be a rather odd collection of people. It included a lad whose fair hair and blue eyes meant Jed would have mocked him as 'pretty' by in his previous life.

'Bit young to be out and about.' Jed sidled up to the lad.

The boy ignored Jed and walked faster to get away from him. Jed caught him up. 'Bit of a nerd, are you?'

'Shove off.' The lad swerved away.

'Just thought, you know, we could be friends.' Jed had developed a cool sarcastic voice that he used when trying to humiliate those he considered weak.

'What?' The lad stopped and looked at him with such scorn, it almost made Jed blush. 'You like bullying people? Makes you feel big? You do know people like you bully others to cover their own weaknesses.'

'Leave it out. You've picked the wrong person. I'm only trying to be friendly.'

'And I don't need self-satisfied, smug bullies to be friends with, thank you.'

'Go and play with the girls and their dolls then.' Jed's look was contemptuous. The lad stopped and his fists clenched. His eyes blazed, but he turned on his heel, and walked away.

'Too scared to fight, hey.'

'Stop it, Jed.' Melanie walked over and gave him a shove. 'Try making friends, not enemies.'

'Pathetic. That's what he is.'

'You're even more of an idiot than I thought.'

Jed scowled at Melanie, then pushed past her. 'Give a bloke a bit of space, will you?'

Melanie's expression said it all – plonker.

One of the older ladies tiptoed up to Jed and laid a hand on his arm. 'I do think it's important we try to be kind to one another, don't you?'

'What?'

'You never know who you may end up having to walk with. Kindness. Always best.'

The look on Jed's face was anything but kind, and Melanie nipped over, smiled at the lady, and steered Jed away from her. She whispered in Jed's ear, 'try not to upset everyone. Especially on your first day.'

'Stupid old cow.'

Fortunately, that group soon decided to follow a different path, but Melanie was adamant that she and Jed stuck to the Way that followed the 'Home' direction on her compass.

'Thought we had to be in a group.' Jed's voice oozed sarcasm.

'We do, but the way you're carrying on, we'll be better off alone for a while. We'll be okay.'

They walked on. 'Bit of alright this,' Jed said as he admired the view over a beautiful part of woodland countryside. They came around a bend, and saw a large shop, standing alone, surrounded by pine forest, decorated with Christmas lights that twinkled and flashed even in broad daylight.

Jed stopped to look and grinned. *I love Christmas. Or I used to.* A sour look replaced the smile.

Melanie was about to try to hold Jed back, but something halted her, and instead she let him amble forward. Outside the shop was a tiny person dressed as a Christmas elf.

'Start your Christmas shopping early. Wonderful bargains. Everything you could need for a hassle-free Christmas.'

A steady stream of people were stopping to admire the eye catching window displays, and then urged on by the elf, they stepped inside. Jed slowed down, and adopting an unconcerned look, he too stopped and eyeballed the display. It was impressive; gadgets, tablets, watches, drones, kits, designer clothes, the latest trainers - in fact anything that a discerning young man might want to add to his Christmas list.

This is definitely a place to check out.

Melanie stood back as Jed sauntered towards the door, smiling at the elf with the confident smirk he had mastered. Out of the corner of his eye, he saw a family with small children gawping at the window. For a moment he could have sworn that the window display was full of toys and games, but as he turned his head, there were all the technogadgets and clothes he had seen earlier.

He scratched his head, but continued inside. The shop was decorated with two enormous Christmas trees, lights flashing and covered in tinsel and baubles. From the ceiling, Christmassy mobiles of angels and Santa Claus twirled in a gentle breeze that wafted the warm smell of mince pies around the store. Shelves groaned under the weight of gifts and garlands. Four large, stuffed reindeers with enormous eyes and curling, fluttering eyelashes sang Christmas songs that filled the entire shop with their music.

Around the door stood a bevy of youngsters dressed as elves, as well as man dressed in a Christmas soldier outfit with a neatly clipped moustache, and not a hair out of place, under his tall red hat. Assistants around the shop wore all sorts of Christmas outfits with flashing bow ties, Santa hats and dangling, glittering earrings.

A woman dressed in a red and green outfit embroidered with holy leaves and pairs of bells, sidled up to Jed. 'Intelligent fella here.' She turned to leer at his colleagues.

'O yes,' said a clipped voice that sounded as if it were used to giving orders and having them obeyed. It was the soldier. 'Here's someone who knows his own mind.' He smiled that made his moustache crinkle at the edges.

'Over to you, Captain Noel,' the woman said, with an admiring look.

'Would you care to step this way, young sir?' Captain Noel said in a voice that brooked no arguments, and pointed Jed to walk in front of him. Jed needed no encouraging because as they walked into a dark corner of the shop, the lights came on. Jed's eyes opened in greedy anticipation as he gazed at the walls loaded with the same gadgets and tablets that Jed had seen outside in the window. At the far end was rack upon rack of clothes, and beyond in a smaller room, were shoes, boots, trainers, sneakers ranged along the walls, with low stools ready for customers to sit and try them on.

'Come in here when you're ready,' said a young woman indicating the array of footwear on offer. She was wearing a red dress covered in white twinkling stars with a silhouette of Santa sitting in a sledge driving his reindeer across the sky.

'Where shall we start, sir?' the soldier asked. 'Tablets, headphones, watches?'

'Um. Those please,' Jed said, pointing to an expensive pair of headphones that he had coveted for some time. The soldier handed them to him and asked what music he liked. He quickly set up a tablet with the music and handed the headphones to him.

'The quality is outstanding.' Jed's eyes shone. 'How much?'

'We don't worry about price at this point.' Captain Noel's voice was soothing. 'Shall I set up an account for your purchases?'

'Suppose so.'

The soldier's smile was tight, and his eyes were hard as they glinted at Jed.

For the next hour, the soldier showed Jed one delight after another, and with no thought for the consequence, he kept adding items to his basket aided by pressure from Captain Noel. Finally, the captain led him to the young woman manning the footwear department.

Having established his foot size, Jed was plied with top of the range brand-named footwear. He selected four different shoes, and the young lady quickly added them to his basket.

'Is sir ready to settle his bill?' The soldier appeared at his side.

'Sure. Maybe I'll have a quick look for something for my mum and sister.'

'Of course, sir. And what might these ladies like?'

'My mum - perfume, perhaps.'

'This way.' Captain Noel led him away to a glass counter, where the fragrance of perfume hung heavy in the air, and a middle-aged lady, heavily made up and wearing a two-piece red suit trimmed in white fur, was presiding over a vast range of scents.

'This young gentleman, having purchased a variety of exquisite gifts for himself, would now like to generously buy some perfume for his mother,' Captain Noel said, winking at the woman.

'Of course. What do you have in mind?' the woman dressed in red asked.

'Dunno. What's good?'

At that moment, Jed caught sight of a passageway towards the back of the shop sandwiched between displays of Christmas cards and boxes full of rolls of Christmas wrapping paper. He wandered towards it as the woman turned her back, while she selected a range of perfumes from her displays.

'What's that?' he asked, pointing to the passage.

'Oh, merely a storeroom.' Captain Noel took hold of Jed's arm to try to turn him away.

'But it's glowing.'

'It's the storeroom light.' The soldier's hold was firm.

Jed, never one to be deterred by the demands of authority, shook himself free, and dropped his overflowing shopping basket. 'I'll have a quick look.'

'I told you, sir. Only a storeroom.' Captain Noel kept trying to turn Jed away, but just as determinedly, he sidestepped around him.

'I really don't think …'

'It's cool. No worries.' As Jed eased himself between the Christmas card display and rolls of wrapping paper, the light glowed ever brighter. It was nothing like the harsh, fluorescent light of a storeroom, but had a soft, yet attractive quality to it. Pure white. Jed tiptoed down a short passage, but as the light grew brighter, a terrible smell grew stronger. It was the smell of a farmyard, and reminded Jed of visits to a local farm to see cattle and sheep when he was younger.

'Phew.' Jed covered his mouth and nose with his hand.

He stepped into a cave hewn from rough stone, and around the edges were wooden cattle stalls, with a straw-strewn floor, and cows leaned over the top bar of the stalls, chewing the cud. Goats peered through the lower bars of some other stalls. In the corner, though was the source of the light.

A young couple, the girl looking no older than those in Jed's class, were gazing with faces filled with awe at a tiny, tiny baby all wrapped up, lying in what must have been a feeding trough filled with straw. On a shelf, a small oil lamp lit the darkness, but the brighter light seemed to emanate from the child himself.

'This is so weird.' Jed looked back towards the Christmas shop, and then again at the scene before him.

The girl looked up at him and smiled. 'Welcome. Have you come to see the baby?'

'Um. Not really. I saw the light and investigated.'

'Come and see. Isn't he divine?' The girl stroked the baby's cheek. 'So soft.' She smiled up at the man. Jed reached out his hand and caressed the baby's face. The baby's eyes opened, and he and Jed exchanged a deep gaze.

At that moment, there was a kerfuffle from the far side of the cave, as some roughly dressed men stumbled into the cave, wearing dirty robes and head cloths held in place with a band. One carried a lamb in his filthy hands.

'He's here. It's the baby.' The leading man turned to those behind him.

Murmurs of awe and appreciation drifted around the cave as the men, one by one, hurried in and knelt before the feeding trough, and gently touched the baby.

'It's true,' one of them said, and turned to the girl. 'We're shepherds. Out in the hills. Tonight, we had visions, visions of angels glorifying Adonai and proclaiming the birth of his son Yeshua. We were told to go and find him.'

'So here we are,' another said. 'It's incredible.'

'We brought you this,' another said, handing the lamb to the man.

'Thank you,' the man said, smiling as he took the

wriggling lamb and popped him into a low enclosure.

For quite a while the shepherds stayed talking to the man and girl, cooing over the baby, and telling and re-telling their story of the angelic visitation. Jed stood there gazing at the scene, shaking his head in amazement.

Later, the shepherds left, clapping hands and shouting about how amazing it was. In fact, they made so much noise that the baby woke up, and the woman lifted him up to feed him.

'What's your name?' she asked Jed.

'Jed.'

'I'm Mary and this is my husband, Joseph.'

Jed went white. 'I thought it was all a fairy story.'

'What is a fairy story?' Mary had a quizzical look on her face.

'A story you tell children but definitely not true.' Jed scratched his head.

'So what was this story for children?' Mary smiled at him and Joseph, who had been tickling the baby's feet, looked up at Jed.

'You. Mary. Joseph. Baby born in a stable, and placed in a manger because there was no room for him at the inn.'

'And now you know it's not a story?'

'Yeah. I mean it was all thousands of years ago. Now I'm here, and you're here, and shepherds and …' Jed's voice trailed away. 'I don't get it. I don't even know why I'm here.'

'Are you a Way walker?'

'Suppose so.'

'People have been walking the Way ever since time began. Choose well young Jed. Always home.'

Jed shook his head, and looked again at Mary, Joseph and the baby. 'Better go. I was in a shop buying loads of stuff. Don't think I need it.'

Mary smiled. 'I'm so pleased you came to visit.'

'Yes, son. Good to meet you,' Joseph said, and tapped him lightly on the arm.

Jed turned around, and with a heavy heart made his way back up the passageway to the shop.

He emerged into the open air. Nothing there. No shop. No Christmas goods. No elves or assistants in Christmas dress or Captain Noel. All was quiet. Just Melanie waiting, playing with the solitaire set, snacking on nuts.

'Amazing,' Jed said.

Melanie nodded, smiled and stood up. 'Come on.'

9 LEARNING TO EARN

For the next few days, Jed and Melanie walked the Way, aligning themselves by Melanie's compass to Home. Jed's direction was never the same, though his eyes were constantly drawn to the otherworldly glow that always seemed visible over the distant mountains.

Each day they walked with a group of other Way walkers. 'Always keep company. Too dangerous on your own,' Melanie had said.

However, groups shifted and changed every day. The Way was not always clear, and different groups all seemed to have their own ideas about which path to take. Melanie insisted they followed the direction her compass pointed.

Along the Way they passed villages and small towns where they could buy food, or anything else they needed. Every night they camped in one of the campsites that appeared at regular intervals.

'Aren't we all going the same direction and to the same place?' Jed asked Melanie one evening.

'No, unfortunately not. Everyone's idea of where home is, and how to get there vary a lot.' Melanie gathered up their dirty supper things.

'How do you know which is the right one?'

'Reading the Way manual and listening to those whose compasses seem to point to the path that the Way manual directs.'

Jed hardly ever read his Way manual though Melanie seemed to be always reading hers. 'Listen to what some people we're walking with tell you. Then check it out.'

The rain, which had begun as a light shower, turned into a heavy downpour. Melanie scrambled into her tent, shoving her things before her.

'Fancy a game of chess?'

'I'll try, but I'm not much good.'

They both huddled into the tent, and Melanie fished out her little games set, and they had a couple of very unsatisfactory games. Melanie beat Jed easily every time.

'Told you I'm not much good,' Jed said, looking embarrassed.

Melanie sighed as she packed the set away.

'I'm going to bed,' Jed said.

'Good night.'

Next morning, they approached a group of people from many nationalities who were preparing to leave.

'Hello. Can we join you?' Melanie asked.

'Of course,' a young oriental looking man said. He was expertly packing up his gear, and then ordered his group to line up ready to walk.

'At least it's stopped raining,' Jed said to an elderly man who looked as if he came from China or Japan. He fell into step alongside him.

'Yes. Not that it has stopped us from getting wet and muddy.' The man scowled and pointed to the young man. 'Our leader tried to make us push too far yesterday, and we didn't arrive here soon enough.'

'That's a pity.' Jed tried to sound sympathetic, but his face betrayed a complete lack of concern.

'Yes, it is. These youngsters have no regard for their elders.'

'Shame.' Jed flicked his eyebrows up. *Old People. Huh.*

'Where are you making for?' Jed asked.

'Home.' The man gave Jed a look that said his picnic was short of a sandwich.

'I believe there's more than one opinion on that.'

'Maybe, but Confucius was a great man who taught men to gain knowledge and be righteous. He said, *"What you do not wish for yourself, do not do to others."* He had much to say about how to live right. We try to follow his ways.'

'I don't think I've heard of him,' Jed said, with a hint of apology.

'Then you would do well to heed his wise words, *"you cannot open a book without learning something"*. Do you read much?'

'Not much. Maybe I'll read my Way manual a bit more.'

The old man sniffed with contempt. 'You will find nothing in that book to improve on the teachings of Confucius.'

'Well, thanks.'

Jed watched as the old man's group turned left and marched up another path. Melanie and Jed were approaching quite a large town. He shrugged and went and found Melanie, who was chatting to an older, very elegant woman. Her hair was pinned in a stylish pleat, and though she wore hiking clothes, they were immaculately clean and well pressed.

'I have always believed the path home is through

good works. They pave the path to the City of Light,' she said.

'Really?' Melanie said. 'The Way manual says we all have to face and cross the chasm.'

'I've never placed a lot of store on the Way manual.' The woman patted Melanie on the arm. 'Lot of writings from men written ages ago. Not relevant today.'

She smiled at Melanie as if she was six years old. 'Personally, I do not think Yeshua wants us to try anything as dangerous as crossing the chasm. It's almost like committing suicide.'

'But Yeshua has already crossed the chasm, and made the Way,' Melanie said, her face blushed red under her brown skin.

'Well, if that makes you happy … personally I am depending on my good works. If I do enough, I am sure I will be allowed into the City of Light.'

'It has nothing to do with making me happy. Wouldn't it be lovely if we all just walked into a perfect City of Light.' Melanie's tone was scornful. 'In that case Yeshua wouldn't have had to die, would he?'

She grabbed her Way manual. *"Surely he took up our pain and bore our suffering,*
yet we considered him punished by God, stricken by him, and

afflicted.

*But he was pierced for **our** transgressions, he was crushed for **our** iniquities;*

*the punishment that brought **us** peace was on him, and by his wounds **we** are healed."*

Melanie's eyes blazed. 'He did it for us. So we could all join him in the City of Light. I'm not perfect, and I bet you're not either.'

The woman reluctantly shook her head.

'The only certainty for people like you and me to reach the City of Light is to cross the chasm, and the only path over the chasm is Yeshua's way. Good works will never do it.'

'Interesting,' the woman's voice had an edge of uncertainty. 'I'd never thought of it like that before.'

'Come on,' one of her companions said. 'Many people to help here.'

The lady re-joined the group of women who laughed amongst themselves as they left, glancing back at Melanie, who glared after them.

'Bit patronising,' Jed said. 'What did she mean about the City of Light?'

Melanie pointed to the horizon where the strange, magnificent glow pulsated with great energy and intensity. 'See that?'

Jed nodded. 'Wondered what it was.'

'That's my home. The City of Light. I hope it will be your home, too.'

'What's so special about it?'

'It's where everything finds fulfilment. It's perfection. It's where we were all created to live.' The look on Melanie's face was one of blissful anticipation.

'So? We all go there?'

'The only means is by crossing the chasm.'

'Who says so?'

'The Way manual.'

Jed's face was a mixture of disbelief and derision. 'The only home I'm interested in is where my mum and sister live.'

Melanie shook her head, her face exasperated.

Jed shrugged. 'I'm starving.'

Melanie took a deep breath and glared at him. 'So am I, but we've no food.'

'Wayfarer bar?'

'No. We're going to need to work soon. My money's almost gone and I'm not sure how much you have left.'

'Not much. Lost a lot at the chocolate place.'

Melanie raised her eyebrows and sniffed.

'What sort of work could we get?' Jed asked.

'Shops. Farms. Babysitting?'

'No thanks. Looking after my sister was bad enough.'

'Really? Let's see what's on offer.'

They walked down the main road of the town, stopping at a shop to buy food with the last of their money.

'Any jobs?' Melanie asked a young lad sitting at the till, wearing yellow overalls with blond hair, and his chin covered in the first down that one day might grow into a beard.

'I'll see.' He looked around but didn't seem to see who she was looking for. 'Peter!' he yelled.

A sour faced man appeared from out the back and glared at them. 'What do you want?'

'These two would like to know if there are any jobs?'

'Yeah, I can use you for a couple of hours to re-stock the shelves. Done any of that before?'

'I have,' said Melanie.

'Not me, but I'll learn,' Jed said.

'You better. Not paying you for a poor job.'

The man explained to Melanie what was required, and left them to it. Three hours later, Jed was exhausted from lifting and pushing boxes of groceries all around the store on a trolley, whilst Melanie actually arranged the contents onto the shelves.

'Okay. Time's up.' Peter reappeared. 'Come to the office, and I'll pay you.'

They followed him to a pokey, dirty cupboard of an office, piled high with boxes and paperwork brimming over every surface, and falling to floor. It smelled, and they tried not to grimace as Peter carefully counted out a few coins.

'That it.' Melanie's voice rose in disgust. 'Slave labour.' She scowled at Peter.

'Take it or leave it.' Peter looked as if he would take the money back, but Melanie closed her fist around the coins. 'We'll take it.' She handed half to Jed. 'Come on.'

Outside Melanie said, 'I think next time we should look for a farm. It's harder work but better paid, and you usually get showers, a bunk in a dormitory and food.'

Jed looked around at the town. 'I'd love a shower and a bunk, so where are we going to sleep?'

'There may be a bunkhouse round one of these corners. No time to get to a campsite now.'

The sun was already setting, and after asking a passing walker about a bunkhouse, they turned down a side street, and found a surprisingly modern, well fitted out accommodation.

'You're lucky. Last two bunks available for tonight. One in the men's and one is the women's.' An elderly man who looked like life had been hard on him, pointed at the two doors. 'Kitchen over there.' They paid for the accommodation, and the man turned away, picking up a bottle and taking a swig from it.

'You're cooking tonight,' Melanie said. 'Risotto?'

'What? I've never cooked that before.'

'Time you did. Met you in the kitchen in 20 minutes.'

10 THE FARM

We need to earn more cash, or we'll run out of money and food,' Melanie said next morning. 'Bunkhouses are great, but far more expensive than campsites.'

'Don't fancy another shop.' Jed scowled.

'Sometimes we have to do things we don't want.'

'Yeah. I'd prefer a nice office job using computers. I'm not cut out for hard labour.'

'Honestly, Jed. You're a wuss.'

'No. I'm more suited for a managerial role. You know telling others what to do whilst I monitor everything.'

Melanie's face was a picture of undisguised incredulity. 'You can't manage yourself, let alone anyone else.'

Jed tried to look offended. 'Hidden depths, that's me.' Jed had his ultra cool expression firmly in place.

'I'm looking for a farm. It's hard work, but worth it,' Melanie said.

Jed pulled a face.

The Way manual took them through countryside dotted with farms. Enormous fields full of grain, turning golden, stretched into the distance, but there were also fields bursting with rows of vegetables, surrounded by neat hedges. Melanie seemed to be looking for a specific place.

'What about this one?' Jed asked as he looked at the sign *Animal Farm*. 'George Orwell and all that?'

'Nothing to do with him. I want to find an arable farm, crops not animals.'

They walked on. 'This looks more promising,' Melanie said as she read the sign *Farmer Tubby's Farmstead*.

'Farmer Tubby! Hope that means loads of food.'

They hurried down the lane that ran between high hedges till it opened out to reveal the most unusual farmstead. All the buildings were circular and had dark brown brick walls with roofs that were conical, and creamy coloured, often with a pinnacle on top. A few had no walls, the roof supported by pillars, and from which hay bales spilled in untidy cascades into the yard.

Doors and windows were round or shaped like arches, and the tantalising smell of pies and bread wafted over the farmyard.

'This is a bit more like,' Jed said.

At that moment, the fattest man either Melanie or Jed had ever seen, waddled out of the main house. He wore a green and red tartan kilt, held up by braces over a white T-shirt and with a tam-o'-shanter on his head.

'Welcome, welcome,' he said with a broad grin on his face, and a strong Scottish accent. He took each of their hands in his pudgy fingers. 'Everyone is welcome here as long as you have come to work.' He slapped Jed on the arm. 'Only workers eat. Wages are fair.'

'Come this way.' He took them to a pair of bunkhouses, round and with conical roofs. 'Lads there and lassies to the other one. Come round the back of the homestead when you've dropped your things, and we'll give you a drink before setting you to work.'

Later, Farmer Tubby showed guided them to fields to pick pea pods hidden amongst tangled stalks supported by twigs. Around them a small army of other workers picked peas, pulled carrots, onions, parsnips and swedes, and some were working along drain pipes, supported on wooden trestles, filled with overhanging strawberry plants. The juicy, red fruit hung in clusters making picking much easier than those with the backbreaking task of pulling carrots and parsnips.

The farm seemed to grow every conceivable fruit and vegetable, and Jed imagined there would be work here all year round. The thought of all those pies and bread that he had smelled earlier made his mouth water. However, hard work was not Jed's idea of life. He picked a few pea pods, and dropped them in his basket, and when Melanie's basket looked much fuller, he grabbed a handful, and popped them in his own.

The second time he did this Melanie complained loudly to him. 'Pick your own.'

'You've got loads. Can't you spare a few for a mate?'

'Sure, but not one who is too lazy to do their own work.'

Jed moved away from Melanie and tried nicking the pea pods from others' baskets. Mostly he was successful, but one well-built, muscular fella, seeing what Jed had done, grabbed Jed's entire basket, and tipped it into his own.

'Oi. Give that back.' Jed went and eyeballed the fella, who stared back without flinching.

'Got a problem?'

'Yeah. You took all my peas.'

'I don't think they were all yours, sonny.' He handed Jed his empty basket. 'Work.'

By the end of the afternoon, Jed had half a basket full of pea pods. He discovered that the peas inside were very sweet and tender, and he ate quite a lot, hiding the pods amongst the plants.

Farmer Tubby stood by the farmstead, with a clipboard in hand, making notes of who had picked what. Jed's mouth opened in disbelief when he saw Melanie's five overflowing baskets. Everyone else had so much. His face was bright red when he presented his half full basket.

'You haven't been putting much effort in have you Jed?' Farmer Tubby said. 'Remember, I told you if you don't work, you don't eat.'

'Yeah, but that fella stole all my peas, and put them in his basket.' Jed's whine was worthy of an Oscar for piteous acting.

'Of course, you took no one else's peas, nor ate any either?'

Jed blushed an even deeper red and looked at his feet.

'You'll learn, young man. You'll learn.'

Everyone went into the dining hall and sat down in

places that had nameplates by them. Jed rubbed his hands in anticipation as plate after plate emerged with a steaming pie, and a pile of vegetables. Jugs of gravy were placed on every round table.

Finally, a tiny plate with a minute pie and a few raw peas was placed in front of Jed. 'What? Where's my pie?' He pointed to all the others round the table.

Farmer Tubby called from the far side of the room where he was tucking into a huge pie. 'I told you Jed. If you don't work, you don't eat.'

Jed nibbled his pie and peas, trying to make it last. He was starving. 'Don't feel like giving me a bit of yours do you, Melanie?' He gave her his most optimistic, winning look.

'Sorry. Can't. House rules.'

After supper, Farmer Tubby called to Jed to follow him. He led him out to the stables where every stall housed a horse, but one much tubbier than normal. Their legs were rather short for their round tummies that hung close to the ground, and their manes, though groomed hung over their eyes so they peered through the hair at anyone coming in their direction.

'This is a second chance for today. Feed and water the horses, and you'll get a small, late supper.' Farmer Tubby eyed him up and down. 'Do a poor job, and you'll leave the farm in the morning.'

'Okay.'

'Jess will show you where everything is, and I'll be checking with her how you get on.'

Jess, her hair tied back in a ponytail, and wearing jodhpurs, long brown riding boots, shirt and green, quilted gilet, led Jed to a tap with a bucket hanging under it. 'Fill the bucket, take it to each stall. Open the door and fill their water trough. Watch out they don't kick you.'

'Thanks.' Jed glowered at her. 'Never been near a horse before.'

'Great opportunity to learn.' She turned away and entered another stall. 'I'm going to be grooming. When you've watered the horses, I'll show you where we keep the feed.'

Jed filled the bucket, walked to the nearest stall, and opened the door. The horse looked at him, its head on one side.

Jed eyed the horse with deep suspicion. 'Hello horsey. Good girl.'

Jed edged into the stall spilling water on the floor in his attempt to avoid a kick from the horse. Instead, the horse sidled over to Jed, crossed its hind legs, and leaned on him, squashing him against the wooden wall of the stall.

'Oi. Stop that.' Jed pushed the horse, which merely squashed him even more. 'Help! I'm being crushed by this horse.'

The door opened, and Jess stood there laughing. 'Milly is only being friendly.' She tapped the horse's rump. 'Stop it Milly.'

The horse turned around, gazed at Jess with innocent eyes, and stood upright.

'Tip your water in the trough before you lose any more,' Jess said.

After successfully filling Milly's water trough, Jed opened the door of the next stall. A large but rotund stallion glared at Jed. Its hind hoof scraped the ground.

Jed inched into the stall, holding up his bucket so the horse could see he was bringing water.

The horse grazed its hoof again across the floor.

As Jed sidled alongside, it gave a great kick of its rear hoof against the closed stall door. Jed jumped, and more water sloshed out of his bucket.

'Major. Behave.' Jess's voice wafted from another stall.

Tipping the leftover water into the trough, Jed hurried out of the stall, clinging close to the wall.

'This is life threatening.' Jed yelled at Jess.

'Nah. They're not good with strangers, that's all.'

'So why am I doing this?'

'I gather you weren't very keen on picking peas today.'

'No. Not my strength. I'm more managerial.'

'Not much call for managers on this farm. Just workers.'

'Hmph.'

In the next stall, Jess was plaiting a beautiful, glossy black mare's tail. She had already plaited the mane in coils along its neck.

'Kelly is going to a gymkhana tomorrow. Show jumping.'

'She'll never jump any fences,' Jed said looking at her rotund girth. 'Knock them all off.' He laughed as he went to empty his bucket in the trough, but then yelped as Kelly gave him a sharp nip on his backside.

He turned round with fist raised ready to thump the horse, which opened its eyes wide in an innocent gaze.

'What d'you do that for?' He glared at the horse.

'I did warn you. These horses understand you,' Jess said.

'Stupid animals.' Jed stomped out of the stall.

Jed continued filling the water troughs. The last stall had a rather small, skinny bay pony that had terrible scars along its back. It skittered nervously as Jed opened the door.

'It's alright,' Jed said, as he tiptoed into the stall. He put his hand out to touch the scars, and the horse flinched. 'What happened?'

The horse eyed him, fear in its eyes. Jess appeared, and softly said, 'Farmer Tubby rescued Beauty. Her owner was treating her dreadfully. He had to pay a lot for her, but he can't stand cruelty to animals.'

Jed emptied his bucket, and then carefully stroked Beauty's neck, and ruffled her ears.

'She's hardly eaten yet,' Jess said.

'It's alright girl. I won't harm you,' Jed whispered.

'You still have to feed them, Jed.' Jess held out the open stall door and with reluctance, Jed left Beauty.

He was ready now and knew what to expect as he opened each stall door with a bucket of feed. He talked to every horse by name, and he was soon back filling Beauty's trough. He again stroked her neck and whispered kind words into her ears.

'Well done, young Jed. You've earned some supper.' Farmer Tubby stood by the door out of the stables. 'Would you like to work with the horses tomorrow?'

'Yes. I think I would.' Jed smiled. 'Never been near a horse before, but I enjoyed it. Kelly bit me.'

Farmer Tubby laughed. 'What did you say? You'll have to learn to speak well to the horses.'

For the next week, Jed worked every day in the stables getting to know the horses and how to look after them. Jess showed him how to groom them, and when Kelly reappeared from her gymkhana with a rosette, Jed was delighted and patted her neck enthusiastically.

Much to Jed's delight, Jess also started to teach him to ride. By the end of the week he could walk, trot and canter round a field, usually riding Milly.

As day followed day, what delighted Jed most was Beauty, who no longer edged nervously away from him, but welcomed him by nuzzling against him when he entered her stall. He spent as much time as possible with her and began to bring her treats. After holding out a juicy apple in his open hand, Jed smiled in delight when she chomped it down without trying to get away from him.

He rushed out of the stall and found Jess. 'I think Beauty is recovering. She's not nearly so nervous. She just wolfed down an apple.'

Jess opened the stall door with great care and went and ran her hand down Beauty's neck and thigh. Beauty snickered gently. 'I think she really is on the road to recovery. Well done, Jed.'

Jed smiled, not his Mr Cool one, but with a genuine look of pleasure.

'Pity you're leaving tomorrow,' Jess said. 'I'm leading a trek out, and you could have come too.'

'Yeah. Melanie wants to get back on the Way. I'll see if we can delay one more day.'

'You could stay here permanently. I'd be happy for that.'

'I'm torn. I'd love to stick around here. It's been amazing looking after the horses, and I'm going to miss them, especially Beauty, but Melanie's been good to me, and I think I ought to go with her.'

'Way walkers. Always onwards and upwards.'

'Yeah.' Jed glanced up at the distant mountains and the ethereal glow from the City of Light that seemed to get nearer and brighter. Something stirred in his heart, and with a deep sigh he said, 'Sorry. Need to get back to the Way.

City of Light

11 THE CITY

Melanie and Jed left Farmer Tubby's Farmstead with heavy hearts, full stomachs, and a pocketful of cash. Melanie had delayed departure so Jed could go on the trek, which had been one of the most enjoyable events of his brief life.

There were quite a lot of tears as they said goodbye, and Farmer Tubby had hugged Jed in a warm embrace. 'You've done well, lad. Beauty will miss you.'

'I'll miss her too.' *Dreadfully.* In fact, when Jed had said goodbye to her, his eyes had filled with tears, and Beauty had nuzzled his hand as if sensing he was leaving. Jed had stumbled out of the stall, and flicked the tears from his cheeks as he joined Melanie.

'That was fantastic. I'd have loved to stay,' Jed said, as he and Melanie stood by the junction of the main path, hoping a group would pass by soon.

'Why didn't you?'

'That place.' Jed pointed to the glow over the mountains. 'I think I want to go there.'

Melanie looked surprised, but pleased. A small group of five people, three men and two women, strolled along at that moment.

'Want to join us?' the leader of the group said. 'Tim.' He held out his hand to them. He wore casual clothes, but it was easy to imagine him in a business suit, chairing a meeting. He introduced the rest of the group. 'This is Jan,' he said, pointing to an elderly lady, 'and this is Sahila.' Sahila was Indian, dressed in a sari, who tilted her head in a gracious nod.

'These two fellas are Ian and Geoff.'

Tim's eyes smiled warmly at Melanie, but as his gaze rested on Jed, his face said, "don't mess with me, son".

Jed studied him back with suspicion and hostility and thought of his dad. His stomach churned as he remembered how he had totally trusted him, and the crushing depth of his disappointment when he walked out. Could he trust Tim?

As if sensing his thoughts, Jan came and took his arm as they walked. She was petite, a word his mother used to describe herself. She believed it made her sound more interesting than plain old short or small. His eyes were wistful as he thought of his mother. Would he ever see her again?

'Penny for them?' Jan asked.

Jed shook his head. He turned and smiled at her, taking in her hiking trousers, sensible jumper and coat and boots that looked rather large for her petite stature.

Their journey took them through pleasant farmland, and then out into the countryside. The trail wound through hills and valleys with beautiful views. Streams ran splashing and gurgling down the hillside to join rivers that meandered through the valley floors watering the ground, so it was green and verdant. Brambles covered the hedgerows, and everyone picked blackberries as they passed by.

'Even a bench to admire the view,' Jan said, sitting down for a moment.

'Onwards and upwards, Jan.' Ian, an Afro Caribbean, pulled her easily to her feet. Ian made both Jed and Melanie, another petite one, feel very short, as he was well over six feet tall and built for rugby. Melanie squared up to him with a "you don't intimate me" attitude, even though she had to bend backwards to make eye contact.

Jed didn't even try, but gazed past Ian's shoulder, and mumbled 'soccer' to Ian's rugby or soccer question.

Ian smiled at Melanie. 'Bet you're alright in defence. You'd bite a few ankles.'

Melanie laughed. 'Never had the chance. Didn't do

much sport. Didn't do much school, come to that.'

'Yeah, me too. Kicked out to work at 16.' Ian and Melanie high-fived.

Jed looked on, scowling.

'And you, son, made no use of the silver spoon stuck in your mouth. Hm?'

'What?' Jed glared at them and stomped off. *Why does everyone have a go at me? Leave me alone.*

The group continued up a long and arduous climb. When they arrived panting at the top, and stood to admire the view, they were all horrified to see below them, not more beautiful scenery, but a large sprawling city, over which hung a heavy pall of black smoke.

Geoff stared at the view. 'Reminds me of where I was born,' he said, in the homely tones of one from Yorkshire. His hands were rough from years of hard labour. 'Had to work down the mines when I was still a lad. Hard life.'

Jed stared at him. *I seem to be the only one with a normal life.*

Even from a distance, it was obvious the city was not a place of beauty or culture. All that could be seen was street after street of the most ugly tower blocks. Sahila looked troubled. 'We must be very careful and stick together. This is an evil place.'

As the group neared the city, it was noticeable that the tower blocks housed large numbers of people in the most squalid of conditions. The roads were jammed with bicycles, handcarts and people hurrying along deeply rutted streets, and disintegrating pavements. The thick acrid smell of the smoke was choking.

'Even Leeds, in the worst of days, wasn't this bad,' Geoff said, gazing at the view of deprivation and poverty. He scratched his beard and shook his head.

Horses and donkeys, stumbling under heavy loads, plodded along the roads, whipped by vicious men.

One donkey stopped unable to go any further with the heavy burden on its back. The man lashed the donkey to try to make it move, but it collapsed on the ground. It was clear it wouldn't be going anywhere anymore.

Melanie ran and crouched down to stroke the donkey's long ears. 'I'm so sorry.'

The donkey looked at her with its deep brown eyes, before its lids closed, and it breathed its last breath. Melanie stood up and glared at the man as he untied the donkey's load from its body. 'You're cruel.'

'Plenty more where that came from,' the man said,

and he kicked the dead body. 'Useless.'

Melanie turned away, her face blazing with anger, her lips set in a hard line. 'Monster.'

Jed had watched the exchange with more concern than he usually showed as he remembered Beauty. He rather awkwardly squeezed Melanie's shoulders and tried to take her mind off the animals. 'Those tower blocks are gross. They're all exactly the same.'

Melanie took a deep breath. 'Yeah. They're all crumbling as well. Look at those balconies.' She pointed to windows from which balconies hung at crazy angles. 'Someone's even trying to hang their washing from that one. She'll fall.'

They both stood with their mouths hanging open as the woman leaned out, but when they were sure she would tumble to the ground below, she pulled herself back.

'Keep together everyone,' Tim said. 'This is not a place to get lost or be alone.'

As they walked along, men, women and children dressed in filthy rags constantly hassled them. 'A few coins, please,' said one lady, her face covered in sores.

'I find it so hard to refuse,' Jan said. 'I know that if I give one of them even a small coin, they'll inundate us.'

Street children, their growth stunted by poverty, kept trying to pick pockets or stick tiny hands into their backpacks.

'Can't we go another way?' Jed asked Tim.

'Wish we could, but this is the Way.'

At that moment, Jed saw Tobi, his Nigerian classmate from school. The look of surprise on his face gave way to relief. A friend.

'Hey, Tobi.' Jed ran over, and they clasped hands.

'Hey, Jed, where you been?' Tobi took him by the arm to pull him away from the group, and into a side street.

'Friend of yours, Jed?' Melanie asked, following them and trying to grip his other arm.

'Yeah. Melanie this is Tobi, Tobi – Melanie.'

'Where the chick come from?' Tobi looked at Melanie with the same disgust as if he had found chewing gum stuck to his shoe.

'Melanie's cool. Honestly.'

'She don't look no funky-ass to me.'

'And you're crump, man.' Melanie's face was scornful.

'Come roll with us, Jed,' Tobi said.

Jed looked at Tobi with longing. The attraction of being part of the gang was strong.

'I'll find you in a bit, Mel,' Jed said, disconnecting her hand from his arm.

Melanie grabbed his arm again in a tight grip. 'No. You won't.' She glared at him. 'Remember what Sahila said, "We must stick together." You leave me now, you won't find me again.'

'I will.'

Tobi looked at them and sneered. 'She your nanny? Come.' He pulled Jed again.

'Did you learn nothing from the gaming halls? You want to fry your brains for good?' Suddenly Melanie dropped his arm and walked away.

Jed started to follow Tobi, and he was quickly surrounded by more of his old friends, welcoming him back. Little packets of drugs appeared, and he gazed at them, tossing up whether to go back to his old ways.

The look of anticipation on his face said it all, but listening to their speech, looking at the drugs, Jed suddenly felt like an outsider. *Who am I kidding? Was I ever really part of this?*

Smiling, with a hint of apology, he said, 'Sorry fellas. See you around.' He hurried after Melanie.

A torrent of abuse, and mocking catcalls followed him.

He ran down the side road, ignoring the jeering, and back into the main street to rejoin the group. 'Melanie!'

She stopped, her eyes wide in surprise, and grinned. 'Hope for you yet.' They high-fived.

'Yeah. I enjoyed being part of the gang. No one else at school seemed to understand how I felt. They accepted me. No questions asked.'

'Right. Bet you were in some right dodgy stuff as well?'

Jed flushed. 'You're right. Wasn't good.'

At that moment, they heard taunting shouts coming from an alley. A group of teenagers were circling around something or someone, feet flying and mouths scoffing. Melanie and Jed ran over, and Melanie pushed herself into the centre of the scrum, where a lad was curled up in a ball, with hands glued to his ears, trying to protect himself.

'Oi. Clear off. Leave him alone.' Melanie shouted at the group and aimed a kick or two back. Jed tried half-heartedly to pull a few of the teenagers away.

'Nothing to do with you, Way walker.' One of the larger lads glared in Melanie's face and raised his fist to punch her. Melanie ducked the punch, and grabbed the unfortunate victim, before running off with him back towards the main road. Seeing their prey no longer alone and unprotected, the thugs tried to turn on Jed, but aiming a very wild punch and kick that missed, he scurried off as well.

Back on the main road with Melanie, Jed could see that they had actually rescued a Down's Syndrome boy aged about 11. 'They're always picking on me when they can't find anyone else,' his voice trembled, and tears ran down his cheeks.

'Come with us.' Melanie squeezed his arm. 'What's your name?'

'Lucas.' He glanced nervously at them.

'It's alright,' Melanie said, but Lucas still hung back. 'We won't hurt you.'

The rest of their group had turned around a little farther down the road, when they realised Melanie and Jed were not with them. Seeing Lucas with Jed and Melanie, Jan laid a hand on Tim's arm. 'Stay here,' she whispered.

With a huge smile on her face, Jan approached Lucas. 'Hello. My name's Jan.'

'Lucas,' he mumbled.

'Are you okay?'

'Not really. I've no one to look after me. My mum died, and my aunt didn't want me.'

'Would you like to come with us?'

Lucas nodded.

Tim joined them, and looking at Lucas said, 'We need to find somewhere safe to stay tonight.'

'I think there's a hostel for Way walkers a couple of miles away.' Lucas looked nervously at Tim.

'Could you show us?'

'Probably. I should have gone there ages ago, but I didn't want to leave this area.'

'Why's that dear?' Jan asked.

'Grew up here.'

Jan took Lucas's arm, and he led them through the dirt and squalor, constantly glancing around nervously.

'How do places get like this?' Jed asked.

'Too many people, uncaring government, not enough money.' Tim shrugged. 'They need Yeshua, but too many Way walkers don't stop to tell them.'

As daylight dwindled, the shadows lengthened, and everywhere looked even more threatening. Wild dogs started to sniff along the filthy gutters and stared with hungry eyes at the group as they passed. Families and even the beggars and street children disappeared, and gangs started to gather. One started to follow the group down the road, taunting them.

'You need a good cause. You could try us. Happy to take your money off you.' Cackles of laughter drifted after them.

Ian confronted the gang. 'Looking for a bit of trouble, lads?'

'Nah. Thought you might like to make a donation to our good cause.'

Ian waved a fist at them.

'Keep going,' Tim said. 'How much further Lucas.'

'Not sure. I've never actually been this far before.'

Another gang started to follow them with more jeering and mocking. They quickened their pace, but even as they did so, yet another group emerged from the shadows to block their path.

'Going anywhere nice?' their leader said, his voice contemptuous. Fingers stretched out to fiddle with their backpacks and try to undo the zips and pockets. They were surrounded. Knives flashed, and the group darted anxious eyes everywhere.

At that moment, bright torchlight bathed the scene, and a group of burly men marched down the street. One torch lit up Tim's face, and a voice called from behind it, 'Having a bit of bother, Tim?'

Tim peered at the torch, then grinned. 'Is that you, Will?'

'Of course.' As the men with torches approached, the gangs quickly melted away into the shadows. 'You shouldn't be out after dark. Come on, food and beds are waiting for you.'

Laughing with relief, they followed their rescuers, and before long the warm lights of a hostel appeared.

'Honestly Will, you do choose a right rough area to live,' said Tim, as they entered the hostel, and dropped their backpacks on the ground, and rubbed their sore shoulders.

'Just as well. You'd have been dead by morning if we hadn't appeared.'

Jed and Melanie shuddered, and Lucas whimpered.

'Right, beds for the night and washrooms upstairs. Ladies first floor. Men on the second. Food in 10 minutes.'

Everyone grabbed their backpacks, rushed upstairs, and found a bed, and then hurried into the bathrooms for a quick wash.

Lucas stood there, shivering and glancing around. 'I'm not with them. They just rescued me.'

Will draped his arm around his shoulders and smiled. 'Come with me. We have a special place for people like you.'

Lucas didn't move. 'What do you mean?'

'Don't worry. We have a lady called Tracey who loves lads like you.'

He led him to the back of the hostel and opened a door into a warm room with about twenty girls and boys noisily playing a game. 'One more for the family, Tracey.' Bill pushed Lucas forward. 'This is – what's your name?'

'Lucas.'

Tracey folded him into a big hug. 'You're so welcome.' She called to another boy. 'George, come and show Lucas where he can sleep, sort out some bedding, get a wash. Supper in 10 minutes.'

'Hey Lucas.' A lad who was smaller than him grinned, and took him away.

'We're going to have to build more space if Yeshua sends us any more,' Tracey said to Will.

'I know. Another five arrived tonight. Will there be enough food?'

'We've never gone short before, no matter how many turn up,' Tracey said.

Will shook his head. 'Another miracle.'

12 THE GARDEN

Jed woke from a deep sleep, in the middle of the night. A man stood at the bottom of his bed. He wore a white robe with a gold sash. His hair was white, and his face was full of life and love.

'Come,' he said.

'Where?' Jed stared at him, with eyes full of distrust. 'I don't know you, do I?'

'No, but I know you, Jason Edward Dawes.'

'Who are you?' Jed pulled the covers tightly round his neck and peered up at the man.

He came and crouched down by the side of the bed, and took Jed's face in his hands. Their eyes made contact. Jed gasped. 'You're the baby.'

The man smiled. 'I am Yeshua. We have places to visit. Get dressed and come.'

'Why?' Jed eyed him with a huge amount of suspicion, but there was something very attractive about the man so, despite his misgivings about going anywhere with a stranger, he dressed, and together they tiptoed outside into the dark and squalor.

'This place is gross,' Jed said. 'What happened? It's dog eat dog. Everyone seems so cruel.'

'This was not how I created it. In the beginning, this world was perfect. One day it will be perfect again.' Yeshua's voice ached with longing.

'What happened? What went wrong?' Jed asked.

'I'll show you.'

Immediately, Jed was in another place. He gazed around at the most beautiful garden he had ever seen. Trees, some tall and slender, some short and squat stretched towards the sky, surrounded by the most exquisite plants and flowers. All the leaves on the trees and plants were shimmering with life, some an almost violent shade of green, and others gleaming in different hues.

The flowers were the most stunning array of colour, shape and size. Every imaginable combination flourished, exuding life – pinks, blues, yellows, reds, whites, purples and every size from the minutest tiny dots of petals to the most flamboyant, extravagant blooms bursting with energy. It was nothing like the formal gardens of his previous life. Here plants tumbled and jostled over each other, climbing and reaching into every available space.

Fruit hung from the branches of trees, and bushes in all manner of luscious shapes, sizes and colour. Paths wound through the extravagant foliage into shady clearings carpeted in green grass that shimmered in beauty.

Jed meandered along the paths. 'This place is amazing. It's well ... beautiful.' He ran his fingers over leaves that were hanging low and fingered some bright purple, trumpet-shaped flowers. 'Everything feels so alive.'

Yeshua laughed. 'Have some fruit.' He picked what looked like a huge peach with fuzzy skin, but it was blue and yellow.

Jed took it but looked at it with cautious eyes. 'Okay.' He nibbled it, and his eyes widened. 'Whoa. Amazing.' He polished it off with three big bites.

Creatures wandered, skittered, scuttled and flew everywhere – mammals, birds, reptiles and insects. Water trickled through pools and flowed along sparkling streams.

Soon Jed arrived at a riverbank. The water meandered through the garden emanating life. He stood on the bank and laughed as fish jumped high, birds splashed water on their feathers and animals big and small came down to drink from the life giving water.

He laughed, his face an expression of sheer delight,

and he put out his hand and touched Yeshua's arm. It tingled with life. It made Jed want to reach out, and know this stranger. Was this someone he could trust?

At that moment Jed noticed a man and woman tending the garden. They were quite naked, and completely unashamed. Jed blushed as he looked at them, but they were laughing and innocent.

'Who are they?' He turned and asked Yeshua.

'The pinnacle of my creation.'

Jed frowned.

Nearby, two enormous trees stood apart from everything else. They too were covered in succulent fruit, but their quality stood out even from the rest of the incredible vegetation.

'I'll get us some fruit to squeeze into a drink,' the naked man said to the woman. He walked away, picking fruit as he went, and placing them in a basket that he carried over his arm. The woman stroked the ears of a fawn that skittered by and chatted quietly to it.

At that moment, another creature glided up to her. It was the most handsome and unusual creature Jed had ever seen. It stood tall, and though similar in shape to a human, it was covered in iridescent scales that shimmered like a peacock in the sunlight - blue and green with tiny scales of vivid yellow and vibrant pink. It sidled towards the woman, and Jed could hear their conversation. The woman was obviously familiar with this beautiful creature and listened carefully as it whispered to her. 'Did Yeshua really say you couldn't eat from all the fruit trees?' Its voice was smooth and condescending.

The woman laughed. 'No. We can eat the fruit from any tree except that one.' She pointed to one of the pair in the centre of the garden. 'If we eat the fruit from that one we will die.'

The creature scoffed. 'You won't die. The reason Yeshua doesn't want you eating from that tree is that it would make you like him, knowing good and evil. You'd know everything.'

'Really?' The woman's voice had a hint of uncertainty. 'He never said why we mustn't eat from it.'

She went over and stared at the tree with its unusual fruit. 'It looks delicious. Surely Yeshua would want us to be like him.' She picked a fruit and took a bite.

The man reappeared carrying some juice in a beautiful, painted jug.

'Come and try this fruit. It's amazing. So delicious.'

The man frowned. 'We mustn't eat from that tree.'

'No, it'll make us like Yeshua.' She held out a fruit

and shrugging, he too took it, and ate.

Suddenly, Jed felt a terrible sense of doom and loss. The man and woman turned to one another, and their hands flew to cover their bodies. 'We're naked.' Their voices were high pitched with fear, guilt and shame.

'Quick. Grab some leaves so we can cover ourselves.'

At that moment they heard a man's voice. 'Hello. Hello, where are you?'

Squealing in terror, they snatched a few leaves, and plunged into the bushes, and hid. As Yeshua came into view, he called again.

'I'm here,' the man said, and the pair of them crawled out from the undergrowth.

'Why were you hiding?' Yeshua's asked.

'Um …' The man and woman looked down, their faces red with embarrassment. They were trying to rearrange the leaves to cover themselves.

'You've eaten the fruit I told you not to eat, haven't you?' Yeshua's face was so sad.

They both nodded, tears dribbling down their cheeks.

'It's her fault,' the man said, pointing at the woman. 'She gave me the fruit.'

'But that creature there lied to me,' the woman said,

pointing at the beautiful creature which had slunk off into the undergrowth.

Yeshua summoned the creature who strode forth with an unconcerned air, though Jed knew from his own experience that it was in trouble, and trying to make out it didn't care.

Yeshua pointed at it and pronounced. 'Cursed. Forever cursed. You will be cursed to crawl on your belly all the days of your life.' The beautiful creature fell to the floor, its colourful scales faded away to a dull brown, and it slithered off, hissing, into the undergrowth. 'Forever you and the woman will be enemies.'

'This is what will happen now,' Yeshua said. 'Women will suffer pain in childbirth, and men will have to toil hard to produce food to eat. It's no longer going to be easy as it is now, because the soil will be filled with thorns and thistles.'

Then, with fierce determination, Yeshua strode into the undergrowth. There was a terrible squeal, and he re-appeared with a dead antelope hanging from his hands.

'What have you done?' the woman looked accusingly at him. 'You've killed one of your creation.'

'All creation will suffer for your disobedience.' Yeshua's voice was stern. Grabbing the carcass, he skinned the antelope and made clothes for the man and woman to wear. 'Your sin, your nakedness must be covered by the innocent shedding of blood.'

The man and the woman were crying, tears pouring down their faces. 'I only wanted to be like you,' the woman said.

Yeshua took the woman's face in his hands and looked into her eyes. 'My daughter, you are like me already. I made you and the man in my image. You didn't have to do anything to be like me.'

The woman sunk to her knees, sobbing in despair.

'And now I must banish you from my garden.'

The man and the woman grabbed one another. 'Why?' The anguish in their voices would have touched the hardest hearts, but Yeshua gazed at them, his eyes also filled with tears.

'It is for your safety. If you eat from the tree of life, you will live forever with the terrible knowledge of good and evil. That is the most awful life sentence of all.'

Their heads were low, they stumbled from the garden, their paradise.

Jed took several deep breaths as tears trickled down his face. He turned to find Yeshua standing next to him. 'I'm devastated.'

'So were we. It would happen. One day, man would strive for independence not realising all he ever needed was here with us in the garden.'

'Even an animal had to die.' Jed sniffed.

'Sin has to be paid for by blood. Without the shedding of blood, there is no forgiveness for sin.'

'Can it ever come good?'

'A perfect sacrifice will be made, and when all who have availed themselves of that wonderful gift, everything will be renewed and restored.'

13 THE KILLING

Suddenly, the garden and everyone in it faded, and Jed stood in a square in an ancient city. Surrounding the square were stone-built houses, with small windows from which people were hanging watching a spectacle.

An enormous crowd was shouting and screaming at something or someone. Men and women wearing long robes, and their heads covered, raised angry voices shaking their fists, and everyone's faces were full of hatred. Everywhere was dark, not the darkness of night, but a shadowy gloom that made Jed shiver. Violence and blood lust were thick in the atmosphere, and evil hung in the air.

Jed's eyes were drawn to a familiar creature, the once beautiful one from the garden, now a dirty brown serpent, who was now orchestrating events. It had grown enormous since Jed had seen it in the garden, and the gloom emanated from him, like the dark clouds of a gathering storm. All manner of misshapen, grotesque demonic creatures scuttled and flew around, harassing the crowd like irritating wasps, stirring the people to shout, and wave clenched fists.

The noise was deafening.

At that moment soldiers dressed in leather body armour over a knee-length tunic hauled a man into the square. Peering through the gloom Jed gasped, and his stomach churned, making him almost vomit as he realised it was Yeshua. *What's happening?*

Some of the demonic creatures landed onto the back of each soldier, riding them like a horse, urging them to do as they commanded. The soldiers dragged Yeshua to a post in the middle of the square and tied him to it. Jed looked on horrified as he didn't even struggle, but this was no helpless victim, but a man of great dignity. Jed couldn't help feeling that this was all happening only because Yeshua was permitting it. *Weird.*

As Jed watched, his focus totally on Yeshua, the serpent slithered over and wrapped its hideous coils around his head. Jed could hear its mocking tones. 'You are mine now. I have you. You couldn't save anyone, let alone yourself.'

The demonic creatures that had been darting and diving around the square harassing the soldiers and people, turned at the serpent's words, and an evil wave of raucous laughter washed everywhere.

'Do something.' Jed's words, aimed at Yeshua, were urgent, but he just stood there.

The soldiers picked up leather whips each thong embedded with sharp pieces of stone, and they took it in turns to flog Yeshua with as much energy and cruelty as they could. His body soon became covered in blood as every wound to his head, body and limbs gushed red. The soldiers didn't seem to care where their strokes landed. In fact, they laughed if a blow landed on the Yeshua's face. Every lash caused him to cry out in great agony.

All the while the serpent whispered and mocked him. 'Over. It's over. The great king, Yeshua Messiah is going to die. No one to rescue you. All these people you helped, look at them now.' The serpent crowed, a most cruel and ugly sound. The demonic creatures continued harassing the crowd, baying for the blood of Yeshua

'Did you think someone would rescue you? Die Messiah, die.' On and on, the serpent wove its coils around Yeshua, taunting him.

Sitting at a table, an officer had been counting the number of lashes, and when it reached 39, he shouted. 'Enough.' The panting soldiers turned and laughed with one another at the disfigured body of Yeshua.

'Surprised he survived,' one of them said.

'Won't survive the next bit,' another said, and they

cackled together.

Yeshua slumped against the post, gasping for air, and the shouts and yells of the crowd, who had stood with fists raised, turned to disgruntled muttering that the spectacle was over.

Meanwhile, the serpent slithered over to a group of men dressed in fine robes with long, blue and white head coverings, who had stood apart from the rest. Their faces showed great pleasure and satisfaction at the sight. The serpent wound itself around their feet, and Jed could hear it whispering 'Kill. Kill. Kill the Messiah.'

Like puppets, this group repeated the serpent's words. 'Kill. Kill. Kill the Messiah.' They turned to the crowd, and urged them to join in so the shouts grew louder, and they roared in unison. 'Kill. Kill. Kill the Messiah.'

Meanwhile, another group who had stood apart, watching the terrible scene with sobs and tears, yelled in response. 'No. No. Let him live.' It became like rival football teams as they yelled in antiphony. 'Kill. No. Kill. No. Kill the Messiah. Let him live.'

The soldiers were enjoying every moment. They grabbed Yeshua who had fallen to the ground battered, with tatters of flesh hanging from his body, and hauled him to his feet. With ill-disguised pleasure, they dumped a heavy wooden cross on him, and forced him to drag it away out of the city gates, and up a hill.

Yeshua staggered under its weight and the soldiers grabbed a bystander to help. As they passed Jed, his eyes met those of Yeshua, and Jed silently begged him to do something.

Jed ran to join the group of his supporters who had yelled for his life, as they followed the mob in procession up the hill.

'What's happening?'

Tears poured down the women's white faces, and even the men's expressions were a mixture of anger and confusion, their eyes brimming. 'They're killing the only perfect one we know.'

'Perfect? Why?'

'He's the Messiah. The only one who could save people. The religious leaders hate that.' The man pointed to the group of men dressed in long flowing robes. 'They've wanted to kill him for ages.'

'All he ever did was good,' one woman sobbed.

'Why didn't he explain to them he had done nothing wrong?'

'He kept silent. Never said a word,' another woman

said, her voice trembled. 'Why didn't he justify himself?' She shook her head, her cheeks pale. 'Even that spineless puppet, Pilate, has gone along with them.'

Jed looked totally confused. 'I'm sorry I don't get it.'

The woman took his arm. 'It's not over yet. Come.'

The crowd straggled behind the soldiers, cursing and shouting for Yeshua's death, egged on by the demonic creatures that continued to pester the people. Every time one of them seemed to calm down, or even looked like they might leave the mob, a demon, harpy, hag or vampire bat urged them back, and mindlessly they would start yelling for his death.

At the top of the hill, the serpent slithered and glided around Yeshua with its nonstop accusation. 'I'm going to enjoy this. Yeshua, Adonai's son, put to death.' It hissed. 'Finished. That's what you are.' The hissing turning to a grotesque snigger.

The soldiers forced Yeshua down onto the cross, and with huge mallets banged enormous nails into his wrists and ankles, pinning him to the wood. Yeshua grimaced, his face disfigured in agony. Four soldiers grabbed the wooden structure, and hauled it vertical, and then, puffing with the exertion, they dumped the wood into a hole in the ground. Yeshua cried out in excruciating pain at the jolting to his bruised body.

Jed starred in horror at Yeshua suspended on the cross. It was the most pitiful sight. Yeshua, marred by bloody wounds, hanging helplessly.

Jed was speechless and shocked beyond words. He had never seen such brutality.

For hours Yeshua hung there, getting weaker and weaker. The enormous serpent, was winding itself around the foot of the cross, biting his heels continuing its abusive words. Every time though a drop of blood fell from Yeshua onto the head of the serpent, it hissed and jerked back as if struck by a hammer.

Passers-by, egged on by the demonic creatures, hurled insults before continuing their journey. The religious leaders now stood sneering and mocking him. 'He claimed he could save others. He can't even save himself.'

'Jump down if you're who you claim to be,' another one yelled, before turning to his friends with a sniff of condescension.

A flock of crows arrived, and began dive bombing the cross, and squawking their derision at Yeshua. Some tried to peck at the flesh hanging loose off his body.

In an instant, everything went black. It was as if the sun, which had been dimmed, was now switched off. Cries of astonishment rang around the crowd especially from the group of followers. Those who had been throwing insults glanced around nervously. The abuse turned to anxious muttering. The soldiers lit pitch torches covering the terrible scene with a flickering gloom.

The serpent hissed, and looked up at Yeshua, but then renewed its attacks with even greater ferocity. 'You're going to die. You're mine. I knew I'd get you one day.'

The crows stopped dive-bombing and pecking at him, but found perches on the top of the cross, or on the few trees that stood nearby.

Suddenly, it seemed as if Yeshua collapsed under a terrible weight, and words came from his bruised lips.

'What did he say?' Jed asked one of them.

'He was asking why he has been abandoned.'

Yeshua then seemed to gather himself, and with a monumental effort, pushed himself up and cried out in a loud voice. 'It is finished.' Then his body drooped, and he hung his head. He was dead.

Jed fell to his knees and cried. He sobbed as if his heart was broken, for it was. The cruelty, and the appalling injustice overwhelmed him. Why had Yeshua let them do it to him? Even after such a short time, his heart had connected with Yeshua, and now like his father and grandfather he had abandoned him.

Turning to his followers he asked, 'What did he mean when he said, "it is finished"?'

They shrugged, and shook their heads, too bound up in misery to reply. 'It's over,' one man said. 'We thought he was the one, come to save us. Now he's dead.'

They turned to embrace and console one another. Jed saw, through his tears, one of the religious leaders organise a group of men to remove Yeshua's body from the cross.

'What are they doing?' he asked.

One of them pointed to the religious leader. 'He's one of us. I expect they're taking Yeshua to place him in a tomb.'

'He must have a proper burial,' one woman said, taking Jed's hand to join a little procession that trooped off, carrying his body. They walked to a nearby garden where there was a large rock tomb, like a cave. Jed watched as they wrapped the broken body of Yeshua in cloths interspersed with beautiful, fragrant spices, and laid in the tomb.

Outside, the men struggled with all their might to roll an enormous round stone over the cave entrance. It took a huge amount of effort, but finally it was in position, sealing the tomb. Everyone turned and walked away, heads hung low, inconsolable.

14 RESURRECTION

The scene changed. Jed could hear the quiet whispering of a few of the women and saw them scurrying back-and-forth gathering together what looked like more spices and ointments, before slipping out of a house.

Jed followed. It was early morning. There was a faint pink light staining the sky enough so he could see the women hurrying away. He jogged after them, keeping his distance.

They ran out of the city, and to the place where they had laid Yeshua's body. In the early morning light Jed could just make out the garden, and in one corner the tomb where they had laid him. However, the stone that they had rolled over the mouth of the tomb had been moved. The tomb stood open. Jed frowned. *What's happened?*

The women ran over to the tomb, and were whispering amongst themselves, casting fearful glances around them.

'Who did it? Who moved the stone?' they asked each other.

'Where have they laid his body? I bet those leaders have stolen it.'

'This is almost worse than killing him.'

The ladies clung to one another till suddenly Yeshua appeared, silhouetted golden and glorious in the rising sun. He stepped forth onto a boulder that stood out from the foliage of the garden. Everyone stepped back in amazement, with cries of astonishment.

'I am he that lives, that lives but was dead. Behold I am alive forever more.' Yeshua's voice rang out over the city.

The ladies ran and fell at his feet, laughing and sobbing.

'Tell your brothers I am alive. I have conquered death. It has no hold on me.'

The ladies glanced at each other and at Yeshua, and then turned and ran back into the city.

Jed and Yeshua were alone. Yeshua strode over to Jed and looked deep into his eyes.

'Well Jason, Edward, Dawes.'

Jed stared back, his knees knocking, his heart pounding, his mouth dry. He said nothing.

'What is your response? Will you Jed, receive my free

gift; the perfect sacrifice to pay for all your wrongdoing? Will you walk in my Way?'

Jed shook his head. 'What? How are you alive? What are you asking?'

'Will you follow me? Live wholeheartedly for me? Will you become mine?'

Jed frowned, his eyes troubled. 'I don't know.'

15 CHASM

Suddenly, Jed and Yeshua were standing on the edge of a terrifyingly wide chasm. All around was desert; dry, barren, rocky desert. No trees, no plants, no birds or animals. The chasm stretched before them endlessly to the left and the right, with no apparent way across. But as he gazed at the chasm, Jed spotted a narrow piece of wood stretching across the abyss.

There was a strong smell of sulphur like bad eggs wafting up on dense smoke from the pit. Groups of people and individuals arrived, and were creeping along the edge, peering into the depths.

Yeshua's eyes seemed to bore into Jed. 'You will have to trust me, even with your life.'

Jed shrugged. 'What do I do?'

'You must cross the chasm.'

'What? You're kidding!' He stared at Yeshua whose eyes stared back, without blinking, serious.

'No way.' Jed ran to the edge and looked down into the abyss. He hurriedly stepped back as he felt nauseous and giddy. Bottomless was the only word to describe it. Flames were leaping up from the depths, and not only was there the terrible smell but also the awful cries of people drifting on the smoke.

'Please, is anyone there? I'm alone and in agony. Please, someone, anyone, please send water. I'm dying of thirst. Is anyone there? Water, I beg you.' The voice disintegrated into wails and howls of dread-filled terror.

Another voice called out of the deep. 'Here, my subjects. I command you to come to the assistance of your king, your great emperor. Where are my slaves who must serve me? How dare you abandon me? Come at once.'

More voices cried out from the depths. 'Help, please help. I'm in torment. Is anyone there?'

All along the vast chasm Jed could hear the voices of those trapped below in the flames. Jed turned and looked at Yeshua 'Can't you help them? Rescue them?'

'I tried, but all their lives they wanted to have nothing to do with me, to live apart from me, and now they have their heart's desire. I reached out to them, but they ignored me. '

'But it's not too late, is it? Surely?'

Jed watched tears roll down Yeshua's cheeks,

dripping onto the ground. 'I have done everything, but they refused me.'

Jed looked back towards the abyss, and his eyes widened in horror as he watched tiny dots moving down the sides of the chasm. People were trying to cross by climbing into the depths. *They'll never get across. They can't.*

He yelled at the people closest to him. 'It can't be done. You'll fall. Come back.'

'Thanks, but we can manage. We're expert rock climbers,' one man roped to another said, as they progressed in a very confident manner into the abyss.

'I don't think ...' Jed watched as they climbed down, banging in pitons with great skill, attaching the rope, and progressing down the rock face. Jed's eyes widened in horror as one of them slipped, and together they fell, their terrible screams piercing the air. Jed reached out a hand as if to catch them. 'No. Oh, no.'

He ran back to Yeshua. 'Is there no other way?'

'All ways lead to the abyss. Everyone comes here, some to fall to their doom in the depths below, or to walk the wooden way.' He looked at the plank.

Jed scrutinised the narrow plank, and saw that it was actually a cross, but it looked so flimsy.

'There must be an alternative.' Jed looked with fearful eyes to the right and to the left.

Yeshua had not moved. 'There is no other way.'

Despite Jed believing him, he still started to jog along the chasm's edge. It stretched on endlessly as far as the eye could see. He turned around and jogged back in the opposite direction, past Yeshua who stood motionless. Again, the chasm ran into the distance, weaving around obstacles, even hills.

Jed returned to him. 'I don't think I'll bother. I'll stay here, thanks.'

Suddenly, he found himself flat on his back on the floor. It was as if Yeshua had thrown him there. He landed heavily; all breath knocked out of him. 'My death cost me everything so that you could have it all.' Yeshua's voice was stern.

Jed's whole body shook, and his voice trembled. 'Sorry, but it's too hard. Either I fall into the chasm, or I fall off the plank. Either way I die.' Tears shone in Jed's eyes. 'Why does it have to be like this?'

Yeshua did not move, but stared deep into Jed's eyes before stepping back.

Slowly, Jed stood to his feet. 'Alright, I'll walk over your stupid cross.'

Again, an invisible hand blocked his path, and Jed

crashed to the ground. He stood up, glared at Yeshua, and made to dodge past him. 'I said I'll do it.'

He started again towards the chasm, but for a third time he hit what felt like a brick wall and lay sprawled and panting.

'That hurt.' He stood up and stared defiantly at Yeshua. 'I'm going to cross.'

For the fourth time, he attempted to approach the wooden plank across the chasm, but Yeshua blocked him. He tried to duck past him, but he was tossed away, so he hit the ground awkwardly.

Finally, panting heavily, he stood with his hands on his knees. 'Please. Let me cross.'

Yeshua said and did nothing.

'Please. I'm sorry. Sorry I didn't appreciate what you did, even after seeing it. I'm sorry I've been so selfish. I'm sorry I wanted to live life without you. I really, really do want to cross.' He took a wavering breath. 'I so want to be with you in your city, the City of Light.'

Jed looked up at the distant glory and for a minute a magnificent song of love for their King filled the atmosphere, overwhelming the cries of the doomed. 'The anthem of my redeemed ones,' Yeshua said, and he seemed to glow in glorious splendour.

'Please, will you help me? I can't do it without you.'

Yeshua laughed, a gentle sound that was both soothing yet terrifying. 'Approach the chasm, Jason Edward Dawes.'

Jed stepped forward, but as he did so, Yeshua touched his hip. It was like being stabbed. 'Ow. That's painful. What did you do that for?' Jed stepped back, and scowled at him.

'To remind you that you wrestled me, and overcame.'

Jed limped forward, rubbing his hip. 'I can't do this. My hip is too sore, and with this limp I'll fall.'

Suddenly, he turned on Yeshua and ran over, and started to pound him with his fists on his side, on his face, on his back. He even stamped on his feet. 'Why did you make it impossible? I can't do it now. I don't want to fall into the abyss.' He collapsed so his face was buried in Yeshua's shoulder and sobbed. 'I want to be with you in the City of Light.'

Yeshua's arms enfolded him and soothed his sobs. As he stepped back, Jed saw the terrible scars on his hands from the cross.

'No one can cross the chasm unless they accept my help.'

'But I can't. I just can't. I'm terrified.' Jed looked up from his hands into his eyes and saw a vision of Yeshua hanging on the cross.

'You can do anything if I help.' Yeshua's said, his eyes resolute. 'Approach the abyss.'

Jed stood and limped over to the edge of the piece of wood, resting on the side of the chasm.

Suddenly, Yeshua was on the other side. Next to him stood a familiar figure. 'Granddad?' Jed's eyes filled with tears. 'Is that you?'

'Come on, son.' His grandfather's loving voice floated across the abyss. 'You can do it. Keep your eyes on Yeshua. Never look down.'

Jed was shivering and shaking, both with nerves and such excitement at seeing his grandfather. His hip was so painful. *I don't think I can.* Then the words 'you can do anything if I help' reverberated through his mind. Taking a deep breath, he stared at his grandfather and Yeshua standing watching on the other side. He took his first step.

Slow step followed slow, painful step. He gazed at the two of them, but they never moved. Even without looking down, he became aware that he was approaching the crosspiece of the cross.

It's wider here. I'll see how deep this chasm really is.

'Don't look down.' Yeshua's voice was like a breath of air.

Nevertheless, Jed flicked a glance down and

immediately wished he hadn't. The abyss plummeted below him into unfathomable depths. The flames surged upwards, and a fresh cloud of stinking smoke enveloped him, bringing the cries of the doomed. He wobbled, the pain in his hip pierced him. *I'll fall. After all this, I'm not going to make it.*

'Look at me.' Yeshua's voice was a command.

'Steady, Jed, steady.' His granddad's voice whispered.

Jed looked up, fixed his eyes on Yeshua's face, and the world steadied. His breathing was jagged, but it too became calmer.

'Walk forward again.'

Jed obeyed, and after two paces more his foot landed on firm ground. He ran off the plank and embraced both Yeshua and his granddad. 'Thank you. Oh, thank you.'

'You did it Jed. You did it. Well done. I'm so proud of you,' his granddad said.

'I don't think I could have done it without you both.'

'I know, but it had to be your choice.'

'Welcome, child of mine. The heavenly city, my country, awaits you.' Yeshua turned and gazed at the magnificent radiance on the horizon that seemed closer now.

Jed took a stride forward, still limping, and the landscape all around changed from barren desert to flourishing countryside with fields, farms, forest and rivers. Beautiful snow-capped mountains soared in the distance. Jed turned to thank Yeshua again, but he, his granddad and the chasm had disappeared.

'Where did they go? I wanted to say goodbye. I thought I would walk with granddad now.'

'Who?' Melanie asked. She had been sitting admiring the view, and now stood up and smiled.

'Yeshua and my granddad. They were here.'

'You crossed the chasm?'

'Yeah.' Jed was still continuing to look around for them.

'Don't worry. You'll see them again one day.' She gave him an awkward hug. 'How was it?'

'The chasm? Terrifying. Have you crossed it too?'

'Of course.' She punched him on the arm. 'Everyone has to choose to cross the chasm or not.'

'But you found me on the other side. How does that work?'

'Dunno. Yeshua sent me to find you, that's all I know.'

'I'm so glad he did.' Jed took a big, relieved breath. 'So plain sailing now?'

'I wish.' Melanie heaved her backpack onto her back, handed Jed his backpack, and together they set off along the Way.

16 BY THE SEA

Jed's eyes lit up. 'Is that the sea?'

In the distance, the ocean shimmered blue and inviting. The day was hot, and thoughts of a dip in the cool waters were very tempting.

'Yeah, do you fancy seeing it again?'

'Cool, but is it okay to leave the Way?'

'I think so. We're not leaving for good, only taking a bit of a diversion, and I asked Yeshua. It seems okay.'

'Where are the rest of the group?' Jed asked.

'Tim, and Geoff stayed in the city to help Will for a couple of days. The others continued on the Way, and I walked with them. I knew I would have to meet you again, and when I reached that spot, I waited till you appeared.'

'How did you know?'

'Yeshua.'

'I don't get it. He never talks to me.'

'He does. You haven't learned to listen yet.' Melanie smiled at him. 'Anyway, we've all agreed to meet at a campsite near the University. No idea where it is, but apparently we'll know it when we see it.'

'Hmph.'

When they reached the coast, they stood and admired the waves curling oh so slowly before dissolving into a mass of white foam that skipped and bubbled till it came to rest like an exhausted marathon runner along the rocky shoreline.

'Time for a swim,' Jed said.

'Fantastic. I'm so hot.'

They scampered along the path, through low-lying bushes to a bay that lay before them with a beach of white sand, soft and fine. The water was deep blue and sparkling in the sun and on either side of the little bay kelp covered rocks stretched out towards the ocean.

A family was sitting under an umbrella enjoying the day, the children building sandcastles, and the father digging trenches in the sand, and trying to dam the sea. On the far side, a group of men and women were sunbathing, eating and drinking from picnic baskets.

Jed and Melanie waved to them as they dumped their backpacks on the sand and stood staring at the sea.

'Do you think it'll be safe?'

'Yeah, as long as we're careful and don't go out too deep.'

'Great.' They giggled together and started to strip off their clothes. Having no swimming gear, they were happy to swim in the underclothes and T-shirts.

Jed rushed down to the sea and tentatively put his foot in the water. 'Ooh. Cold.' He carried on wading into the water.

Melanie also paddled in, but squealed as Jed splashed her with water. 'Stop!' She splashed him back. 'It's freezing.' She took a few calming breaths. 'But OK.'

Together they waded out and once in deeper, crystal-clear water, with no sensation of currents, they launched out, swimming towards a rock that stuck out of the sea. When they reached the rock, they perched on it before using it to dive in the water. They spent some time climbing out and diving in until Jed puffed his cheeks. 'Come on. I'm hungry and getting cold.'

They swam and waded back to the beach, and flopped down on the sand, letting the sun dry them and their clothes. They took out bread rolls that Melanie had brought, and sat munching, watching the sea and the others on the beach, who were also enjoying the beautiful day.

At that moment, a group of men and women dressed in black robes with white collars strode onto the beach.

'I knew it.' The leader turned to the rest of the party. 'Way walkers enjoying themselves in a most unseemly manner.' The rest of the group tutted in disgust.

'And look at those two.' One woman pointed at Jed and Melanie. 'In their underclothes. Quite hideous.'

'Clear off and leave us alone.' The voice of one sunbather floated across the sand. 'Go and be sanctimonious somewhere else.'

The family was trying to pack up their belongings. 'Don't think you can escape,' the leader said to them. 'You need the discipline of Yeshua to drive out your wickedness. You are a disgrace to his name.'

They reached into their robes, and drew out stout, wooden staves, and began to disperse across the beach in order to beat everyone who had been relaxing in the sun only a few moments before.

'What?' Jed said to Melanie as he pulled on his clothes. 'Who are they?'

'Religious police. They snuff out any pleasure. They don't enjoy themselves and don't want anyone else to either.' Melanie was also getting dressed in some haste.

They dodged about, as they shoved all their belongings in their backpacks, to avoid the staves of two of the men who had come to batter them.

'We've no weapons to beat them back with.' Jed yelled. 'I'm clearing off.'

'No Jed. Grab a bit of that seaweed. Those stalks are tough looking.'

'Why don't we run? Leave them to it.' Jed was hanging onto the other end of a stave, dancing around to avoid being beaten by a man who was trying to thrash him.

'Honestly Jed. You're such a coward.'

Melanie ran to the rocks ducking a blow, and grabbed a couple of seaweed stalks, yanking them free. 'Here.' She tossed one to Jed. 'Go and help.'

Jed waved his seaweed stalk at the two harassing him, blocking their blows, and ran over to the group on the far side, who seemed to be giving the religious police a run for their money. They had grabbed their clubs and were beating them back till the black-robed figures fled. Jed stood back watching. *They're doing fine without me.*

Just then the mother of the family cried out. 'You wicked people. You've injured our son. How dare you!' She was holding her young boy in her arms, and blood was pouring from a wound on his head onto her lap.

'It will teach you not to embarrass Yeshua with your sacrilegious ways.' One of the religious police said, smirking in self-righteousness.

Melanie ran over to help the mother staunch the blood from the wound. 'Jed, come and help.'

Jed hurried over with some others, but again he stood back as the men effectively pushed back the religious group. Seeing that they could not crush the beach parties, the religious police regrouped, and stalked off, chased away by the men with Melanie and Jed bringing up the rear. There were loud mutterings about the disgrace of those who lolled about on the beach, exposing their flesh, rather than reading their Way manuals.

Everyone stood breathing heavily, watching them disappear.

'Clear off!' Jed shouted at the retreating backs.

'Ssh, Jed.' Melanie glared at him. 'They've gone.'

Jed shrugged as Melanie checked with the mother that the child was not seriously injured.

'I don't think so. The bleeding is stopping,' the mother said. 'Those people make me so mad. They hate anyone enjoying themselves.'

Everyone started packing up, ready to leave the beach. Any desire to go back to continue the day stifled by the intolerance of the religious police.

As Jed and Melanie hoisted their packs onto their backs, Melanie glowered at Jed. 'You weren't much help.'

'I was. I hit a few of those people.'

'Hardly. You were too busy saving your own skin.'

She turned away and stomped up the path away from the beach.

Jed trudged behind her before pulling out his compass and re-aligning themselves to the direction Home. 'This way,' he said looking shamefaced, and they tramped off together in silence.

17 MONSIEUR ESCROC

Jed and Melanie set out next day, still reeling from the brutal attack of the religious police on them. They had hurried to a campsite the previous night but had tossed and turned because of the bruises from the staves.

'All we did was swim in the sea, and soak up some rays,' Jed said, as he and Melanie ate breakfast.

'I know. Hope we don't come across those people again.'

As they left the campsite, they joined a group of young people, and started to discuss their opinions about walking the Way.

'I don't think there's any special destination,' one lad said. 'One day you stop walking, keel over, and that's that.'

'What's that then?' Melanie pointed to the radiant glow emanating over the mountains on the horizon.

'Trick of the light. All that talk of the City of Light is rubbish.' His voice was contemptuous.

Jed frowned. *That's not a trick of the light.*

'Personally, I think we all get into the City of Light. I mean Yeshua loves us, doesn't he?' the young leader of the group said.

'Dunno. Does he?' Jed pulled a face.

'Course. That's what the Way manual says that your friend has.'

'You read the Way manual too?'

'Nah. Too many dos and don'ts. Personally, I think if it feels good, and doesn't hurt anyone, just do it.'

'Cool. I like the sound of that.'

The lad held out his hand. 'Andy.'

'Jed.'

'Been walking the Way long?'

'Nah. Not long.'

'Walk with us. Always happy to have a new face.'

'Thanks.' Jed grinned.

Soon the paths parted, and Melanie consulted her Way manual and compass. 'This way, Jed.'

'Actually, I think I'll stick with this group.'

'You do know they don't believe in following the Way manual.'

'Yeah. That's cool. I like their ideas. Makes sense.'

'Jed. How can you say that? You've crossed the chasm. The compass points out the direction to take.'

Jed shrugged and smirked. Melanie looked with exasperation at Jed, her shoulders drooping. 'I can't leave you.'

'Why not?' Jed turned his hands, palms outwards. 'I'm a big boy. I can manage,' he said in his most patronising tone.

'All evidence to the contrary.'

'Look Melanie. I'm grateful to you for getting me out of the other messes, but I'm fine now.' Jed smiled. 'Go help someone else.'

'Unfortunately, I'm stuck with you till we arrive at the City of Light.'

'Yeah, well I can manage that alone now, so run away and play with someone else.' He patted her cheek, and gave her a silly grin.

Melanie brushed his hand away. Her face was bright red under her brown skin, and her eyes blazing. She turned and took several deep breaths while Jed, Andy and the others walked off laughing. There were tears in her eyes, which she swept off her face as she turned back to follow them.

'Your little friend is following us. Better behave,' Andy said, loud enough for Melanie to hear.

Melanie glowered, and stomped along behind them, hanging far enough back so she did not have to endure their taunting remarks.

After a couple of hours, they stopped to have something to eat. Most of the group didn't have backpacks, let alone anything else useful like food in them. They all looked expectantly at Jed who, with a show of marked reluctance, shared his food. There was hardly enough for Jed let alone a group of hungry lads.

'See if your friend will give us anything,' Andy said.

'I'll try.' Jed sauntered over to Melanie with his most winning smile. 'Got any food for a friend?'

'Didn't know you were my friend anymore.' She glared at him.

'Course you are. Sorry about earlier. Look you can walk with us.' Jed pointed at the group, who all waved at Melanie.

'No thanks.' Melanie threw a small bag of peanuts at Jed. 'Sorry, all I can spare.'

'Mel! That's not even a mouthful each.'

Melanie shrugged. 'Sorry.' Her face said she was not the least bit sorry.

Jed stomped back to the others and threw the packet of peanuts at Andy.

'Not very generous,' he yelled at Melanie, who ignored him.

For the rest of the day, they ambled along, picking apples off the occasional fruit trees, with Melanie trailing after them until, as the sun was sinking behind the far mountains, they arrived in an area of large, formal mansions each set in expansive grounds. One in particular caught all their eyes.

'Whoa, look at that.' Andy pointed to a huge gateway with large stone pillars on which stone lions sat. On either side of the gateway, an iron railing fence stretched into the distance, enclosing grounds of rolling parkland on which a few deer grazed.

'The gates are open,' Jed said. 'Must mean they want to welcome us in.'

The lads hi-fived, and started, almost at a trot, running along a tree-lined avenue towards a mansion in the distance.

'I'm not sure …' Melanie said, but no one was listening to her. She lagged along behind the group down the avenue, but glanced back anxiously as the gates swung shut, without a sound, behind them.

At the end of the avenue stood a beautiful three-storey mansion, with a rounded roof, little turrets and a tower on each corner.

'French chateau,' someone said.

'What?'

'Looks like a French chateau.'

They all shrugged, and Andy hurried up the steps to the front door and pulled on a long metal handle. In the distance, a bell rang. The group stood around shuffling their feet and shivering, as the temperature had dropped sharply when the sun went down.

Light flooded onto the driveway as the front door opened revealing a butler, wearing morning dress of black jacket and pin-striped trousers. He eyed them up and down with suspicious eyes.

'Oui?'

'Got any work, mate? Bed for the night? Food?' Andy rubbed his hands together and shuffled on the spot.

'Maybe.' The butler had a distinct French accent. 'I will enquire of Monsieur Escroc, the owner.' He shut the door, and left them standing on the doorstep, shivering. Melanie, who was still standing someway away, frowned. As they had hurried down the avenue, she had taken in not only the grand mansion with the formal grounds and parkland but also the high hedge and woods to one side, which created quite a barrier.

After fifteen minutes, the butler returned with a gentleman; everything about him spoke of wealth - tailored clothes, immaculately styled hair, a pair of pince-nez balanced on his nose, and manicured nails on hands that had never done a hard day's work in their life.

'Welcome. Welcome to my home. I am Monsieur Escroc.' He smiled, a cold expression,

Andy stepped forward, his hand outstretched. 'Andy.'

Monsieur Escroc ignored his hand.

'Have you come to enjoy my hospitality for the night, or would you like to earn some money by working tomorrow?'

'Hospitality I think.' Andy smirked, and the others all nodded.

Melanie watched from a distance, her eyes troubled.

'Lancelot,' Monsieur Escroc turned to the butler, 'show our guests where to go.'

He ran back up the steps and closed the door behind him. The butler led them round the side of the mansion, their way lit by low lights spaced along the path. They reached a back door, and Lancelot took them inside up a dark passage, lights coming on automatically as they went, till they arrived at a cloakroom.

'Bags here, if you have one.' Lancelot opened a storeroom door, and those that had backpacks threw them inside. He locked the door. 'For security.'

'Clean up, and I will be back to show you to the dining room.'

'Bit of alright, hey?' Andy jostled Jed.

'Yeah. Hope the food is good.'

'Bound to be.' Andy looked at Melanie. 'Cheer up, darling. Look like you're going to a funeral.'

Melanie glowered at him as she washed her hands and tidied herself up.

The butler reappeared and led them into a large dining room with a high, carved ceiling, and beautiful paintings hung from the walls. The thick and luxurious velvet curtains were drawn, and a welcoming fire blazed in the grate.

In the centre of the room, an enormous dining table laden with crystal glasses, silverware, bone china crockery, and starched white napkins had been set for about a dozen people. The butler showed the group to their places, and at that moment Monsieur Escroc entered the room with a beautiful lady, exquisitely dressed and groomed, and three older children, all wearing expensive designer clothes.

'My family,' Monsieur Escroc said, but with no further introductions. The family ignored the guests.

Half a dozen servants, wearing dark suits and white gloves, came into the room carrying trays which they placed on the long, carved sideboard, and from there they served those seated at the table. Monsieur Escroc and his family first, then Melanie, followed by all the lads who had been walking together that afternoon.

A servant placed a plate in front of Jed. 'Prosciutto tortellini, sir.' On the plate were deep-fried tiny tortellini and with a bowl of tomato sauce to dip them.

The lads grabbed the tiny pasta balls and stuffed them in their mouth. Jed, with some memory of manners from his mother, picked up a fork, and dipped each of tortellini in the tomato sauce. 'Delicious.'

Even Melanie appeared to be enjoying the food. Monsieur Escroc chatted quietly with his family who continued to snub everyone else.

Servants cleared away the plates, filled the wine glasses, and placed the next course, a clear consommé in front of each of them. The lads grabbed a spoon and slurped the soup into their mouths. Again, Jed picked up his soupspoon, and carefully sipped each mouthful.

'My grandparents took us all to this posh restaurant for my grandmother's birthday. This place reminds me of that. We all had to eat properly,' Jed murmured to Melanie as he sipped his wine. 'This wine is amazing.'

'Go easy. This place gives me the creeps,' Melanie whispered, filling a glass with water from a jug.

As each amazing course followed first fish, then an entrée, the lads drunk more and more, their voices rose, and they became sillier and sillier. Jed was feeling slightly woozy, and remembering the gaming rooms, switched to water.

After a delicious course of veal piccata, there was a pause in the food. The lads were yelling stupidities to each other, and Monsieur Escroc signalled to the butler. 'Take them to the accommodation for the night.' He smiled at Jed and Melanie. 'Please stay and enjoy dessert'.

The servants took each lad by the arm and hauled them, none too gently, out of the room. They were laughing and shouting all the way down the passage until their voices could be heard no more.

'Excuse me. Where is the ladies' room, please?'

Melanie asked.

'Lancelot. Show the lady to the bathroom.'

Melanie stood up and followed Lancelot out of the room. Dessert appeared, a beautiful selection of ice creams and sorbets crowned with a wafer. Jed scraped the last of the ice cream from his crystal glass bowl and looked around. *Where's Melanie?*

Monsieur Escroc also looked at the empty place, and waved Lancelot over, and whispered something to him. The butler disappeared, but reappeared soon, and leant over to speak quietly in Monsieur Escroc's ear.

'You had better find her and fast.' He glared at Lancelot, who looked terrified. He beckoned another servant and glanced at Jed. 'Take this one to join the others.'

The man came and grabbed Jed's arm, and dragged him out of the dining room, and down the passage, and out into the yard. 'Melanie? Where are you?' Jed screamed.

The servant, who was surprisingly strong, clamped a hand over Jed's mouth. He continued to drag a struggling Jed away from the house. Out in the yard, Jed saw two large cages similar to those that house lions at the zoo or circus. The lads were inside one of them, mostly lying in the dirt and sound asleep, judging by the snores that echoed round the yard.

The servant flipped a key from his pocket, and opened the other cage, and shoved Jed inside.

'They will collect you in the morning,' he said, as he locked the door of the cage, and without another look, marched back to the house. Jed landed heavily in the dirt, and rushed up, and grabbed hold of the bars.

'Oi! You can't lock me in here. Who'll collect me in the morning?' He rattled the bars, but they were immoveable. 'Oi! Oi!'

The servant completely ignored him.

'Hey fellas,' Jed yelled to the lads in the other cage. 'Wake up.'

The only response was groaning. Andy lifted his head. 'Sorry mate. Should've listened to your friend.'

Jed took a deep breath and kicked the cage bars. 'What are they going to do with us, Andy?'

'Dunno. Forced labour, maybe.'

'Great. You dragged us into a right mess.'

'Don't remember you trying to stop us, or complaining about the food.'

They scowled at one another. Jed looked around the

dark yard. 'Melanie. Melanie. Where are you?'

He sat down, his head in his hands, and moaned. After a while, he dozed off, but feeling very stiff and cold, he stood up to hobble round the cage to try to get his circulation going.

As the grey light of dawn started to illuminate the scene, a horse-drawn cart trotted into the yard. Two horses bearing the scars of frequent beatings stood motionless, their breath blowing out in white clouds into the cool, morning air. Everyone in the cages stirred, groaning and rubbing sore heads and limbs.

On the back of the cart was a large cage, similar to the ones in which the lads were imprisoned. Two muscular, surly faced men jumped down from the cart, and strode over the cage with Andy and the other lads. They unlocked the cage, and grabbed two of the lads, and forced their arm into an arm-lock behind their back. Locking the cage again, they pushed them across to the cage on the cart and threw them inside. They came back and repeated the process until they had transferred all the lads from one cage to the other.

Jed had watched this, his face anxious and calling out to Melanie to come quick and save him. Next, the men tried their key in Jed's cage, but it didn't seem able to unlock it.

'What's wrong?' one of them asked.

'Key's no good.'

The man shoved his companion to one side. 'Here. Let me.'

Jed stood as far back as possible in the cage as the men tried again and again to unlock the door.

'We'll come back later and get you,' the man snarled at Jed, who was shaking and shivering with both cold and terror.

The cart shot off with the men whipping the two horses into a canter, and Jed watched as it disappeared, and the pitiful cries of the other lads faded into the distance. Jed sank down, his head in his hands, and tried not to cry.

Unseen by Jed, at the edge of the yard near the storage sheds, a shadow moved and tiptoed over to the cage. 'Jed. Jed,' the voice whispered.

Jed looked up. 'Melanie!' he yelled.

'Shut up, you prize plonker!' Melanie hissed at him. 'Do you want to get out, or get me captured as well?'

'No. Just glad to see you.'

'Well, I am certainly tempted to leave you here, idiot.'

'You're a right sanctimonious old cow, aren't you?'

Jed's eyes blazed at her. 'You are so certain you are always right.'

'That's because it's not hard when I've been saddled with an A1 moron.'

'I hate you holier than thou goody goodies.'

'And I'm not very keen on stupid jerks, either.'

The whispered argument grew ever more hateful until they both stopped as they ran out of insults. They glared at one another.

'Are you going to get me out?' Jed's lips were tight in a hard line.

'Don't see why I should. You got yourself into this. Get yourself out.'

Jed whined like a squeaky gate. 'Thought you were supposed to help.'

'I never realised I would be dumped with such a fool.'

They stood on either side of the cage bars and glowered at one another as the sun rose.

Melanie inhaled loudly. 'What happened to the others?'

'They were taken away on a cart. They're coming back for me.' Jed looked at Melanie like a puppy who has been told off. 'Please get me out.'

Melanie shook her head in exasperation. 'It was listening to Andy's "I know best" that got us here.'

'Yeah, sorry Melanie. Right as usual.'

The cage bars shimmered for a moment.

She took a deep breath, and looked at Jed, her eyes exasperated.

'I'm really sorry Melanie.' He grinned at her. 'Get us out. Please.' Again, the cage bars wavered.

'Honestly. I don't know how. I've no key.'

'Wrestle that butler chap, Lancelot?'

'Hmm. Any better ideas?' She looked at Jed and puffed her cheeks. 'I'm sorry too. I was horrible. Frustration overcame me.'

Again, the bars guttered like a candle in a breeze.

'Those cage bars are weird.' Melanie frowned at them.

'Are they?' Jed shrugged. 'Seem normal enough to me.' He grabbed hold of them and gave them a shake.

Melanie reached out as if to touch the bars, but her hand passed through them. 'I've heard about this, but never seen one before. I think this is a guilt cage.'

'What?' Jed's tone was derisory.

Melanie stepped forward, through the bars, and joined Jed in the cage. 'This cage is not real. There's nothing there, believe me.'

'Believe me. This cage is very real.' Again, Jed grabbed the bars, and rattled them.

'Honestly. It's an illusion. Look.' Melanie walked right through the bars.

'It's alright for you to perform tricks but not me.'

'Jed. Guilt cages work because you are allowing your guilt to keep you there. You've crossed the chasm. Yeshua took your guilt. It's gone.'

Jed's mind returned to Yeshua's terrible death, and the love that drew him across the chasm.

'I don't get it. These bars are real.' He tapped them, and they rang metallic.

'Jed. Close your eyes.'

He did so.

'Now, step forward six paces.'

With hands outstretched, and his face screwed tight in anticipation of hitting the bars, he stepped forward.

'One, two, three, four, five six.' His eyes popped open, and he stared at Melanie. 'It worked!' He turned around and looked for the cage. 'It's not there.'

Melanie laughed, and they hi fived. 'Told you.'

'Brilliant,' Jed clapped his hands.

'Shh!' Melanie held out her hands, palms upwards. 'You'll wake the place.'

'Sorry.' They laughed and giggled like little children.

'Come on. We need to get away before those fellas return, or Lancelot comes to check on you.' Melanie ran away to the shadow of the sheds where there were two backpacks.

'How did you get those?' Jed asked.

'Came out of the ladies, and the door was open. Grabbed them and ran.'

They laughed again, and Melanie led Jed round the end of the high hedge into the surrounding woods.

'I spent a bit of time last night finding the way out without using the driveway,' Melanie said. 'Follow me.'

With the sun rising, there was enough light to make their way through the woods until they came to a deep ditch with a barbed wire fence running along the bottom.

'How do we get over that?' Jed asked.

'Or under. Which do you fancy?'

'Throw a sleeping bag over the top wire and climb over?'

'Go on then. Let's try it.'

Jed threw his sleeping bag over the top wire to protect his hands and could then clamber over the fence. Melanie quickly followed. Jed's sleeping bag was a bit torn, but it still looked usable. They ran away further into the woods, but as the sun rose higher in the sky, everything grew dark, large rain clouds gathered, and fat raindrops plopped down on them.

'Ugh.' Jed pulled out his coat. 'Let's shelter.'

The pair of them sat huddled under a tree, staring at the rain.

'Any food in your backpack?' Jed asked.

'Honestly? After that dinner.'

Jed laughed. 'You know us lads, always hungry.'

'I've hardly anything,' Melanie said. She found some biscuits and a couple of apples which they shared. 'We're going to need to find somewhere soon so we can buy food.'

Jed pulled a face and glared at the apple as if hoping it might multiply into a fruit bowl.

'Come on. No point in sitting here. We need to get back on the Way,' Melanie said. 'I'm pretty sure I know the direction.'

They trudged off through the dripping woods, heads down inside their hoods, and after about an hour they came across a decent road. Melanie took out her compass, aligned it to home, and they continued, their footsteps growing lighter the further and further they walked from Monsieur Escroc's mansion.

18 THE UNIVERSITY OF THE INTELLECT

For the last two days, a skyscraper, a mass of glass and metal, slender and almost pencil like soared upwards dominating the horizon.

'What is it?' Jed had asked.

'I have no idea. It's so tall yet so thin,' Melanie said, as they sat one evening outside their tents wondering over the strange building.

'How far away is it?' Jed stood up to see if he could at least discover where the oddity met the ground, but too many other buildings surrounded it.

'We've been walking towards it for two days now, and it's hardly become any bigger. It must still be miles away.' Melanie took a bite on a chocolate bar, chewing it slowly.

A man with neatly clipped beard and moustache, returning back from the showers with a damp towel draped over his shoulder, stopped as he heard their conversation. He pointed to the tower. 'The University of the Intellect. Impressive, hey?'

'I suppose so,' Jed said. 'It looks weird.'

'Weird?' the man said, rubbing his damp hair on his towel. 'It's one of the greatest achievements of mankind.'

'Or one of their greatest follies,' another voice said. They all turned to look at the newcomer. He had an extravagant white beard and long hair that almost floated in the gentle breeze. His clothes of ripped jeans and a tattered checked shirt looked incongruous on such an ancient person.

'What would you know, old man?' the other man dismissed him with a contemptuous glance. 'You who have never mined the depths of man's intellect or soared to the heights of his intelligence.' He sniffed. 'What do you know?'

'Enough.' The old man smoothed his wayward beard. 'Whenever men try to build without the foundation of Yeshua, they are doomed to failure.'

'Yeshua! A fairy story invented for the weak minded to salve their feeble consciences.'

Melanie stood up, her face tight and eyes blazing. 'How dare you speak of him like that?'

'See what I mean?' The man's condescending face was more than Melanie could bear. She started to rush towards him, but Jed grabbed hold of her arm and hung on. With a further sniff of contempt, the man strolled off. Melanie's face was red and tight with anger as she glared after him.

'His sort isn't worth it,' the elderly man said. 'Too arrogant for their own good.'

He held out his hand. 'Alfred.'

Jed shook it. 'Jed, and this is Melanie.' He patted the ground next to them. Alfred sat down easing his stiff body to the floor.

'So, what is that place?' Jed asked, pointing to the skyscraper that was now illuminated by myriad internal lights streaming from its windows, as the sun sank below the horizon.

'The university was built to show all the world the height of man's folly, and the depth of his ignorance.'

'I don't get it?' Jed said. 'What's it called again?'

'The University of the Intellect.'

'Isn't that where all the clever people go, and learn to be even cleverer?' Jed's face was puzzled.

'That's what they think. They think they are intelligent, and that going to such a wonderful seat of learning will make them even more intellectual. Hence the name.' It was hard to imagine how Alfred could sound even more sarcastic.

'But it doesn't?' Melanie asked.

'True wisdom, and from that true learning, only comes from Yeshua and his Way Manual.'

Melanie glanced at the book in her hand. 'But this is just one book. There are millions of others to read and learn from.'

Alfred blinked and pierced both Melanie and Jed with a look of such intensity that they leaned away from him. 'All wisdom starts with Yeshua, the King. The Way manual says. You want to be wise. Read this.' He pointed at Melanie's Way manual. 'Only Yeshua can reveal to you his treasures. You won't find those in that place. Man believes he has made significant discoveries. They all came from Yeshua's storehouse of wisdom and knowledge.'

Jed and Melanie stared back at Alfred, looking shocked. 'We've always been told to get a good education, go to university, and then you'll have a fantastic career.'

'By all means read widely from all that is available, study, and even go to these universities. Plumb the depths of man's discoveries of the world in which you live, but realise man is only discovering what Yeshua deposited there in the first place.'

Alfred rose awkwardly to his feet and stretched. 'I must go.' With a brief wave, he ambled off into the darkness.

Melanie and Jed stared at his departing back, their faces shocked. 'Wow!'

For the next few days Jed and Melanie walked with different groups, all of whom had varying opinions and ideas about life, and in particular the imposing tower of the University of the Intellect. Many were stunned at the brilliance of man and his achievements, but a few were not as sure. Like Alfred, they considered that true wisdom and knowledge only came from Yeshua.

'I'll be glad when we find the others. I keep expecting to see them every night,' Melanie said as they turned into the latest overnight campsite.

Almost immediately they saw Jan sitting outside her tent. They ran over and she hugged them both and took Jed's face in her hands. 'Crossed the chasm?'

He nodded.

'Scary, hey?'

Ian appeared and embraced them in a bear hug. 'Good to see you both.'

Sahila then strolled over to join them, a picture of elegance. She smiled in welcome. 'I can see that you have crossed the chasm, Jed.'

'Yeah.'

'The City of Light beckons Yeshua's followers.' They all turned to gaze again at the glorious aurora radiant on the horizon, outshining even the setting sun.

That evening, Tim and Geoff arrived, and it was quite a reunion as they all recounted what they had been up to for the last week or so.

When they departed next morning, the pencil shaped tower dominated the surroundings. Jed murmured to Melanie, 'is the tower stable? It looks like it's swaying.'

'Dunno. I agree it looks very unstable.'

Again, opinions varied amongst the other Way walkers. 'Solid as a rock,' one man wearing a mortar board said. 'It merely moves with the wind. It won't crumble.'

'That is swaying more than would be caused by the wind,' another lady said, who was carrying a bag overflowing with her possessions. She wore a bright red flowered skirt, a hand-embroidered, quilted green coat and on her feet she wore solid leather shoes that looked as if she had been wearing them for a long time. 'I've been walking the Way for years following the teachings of the Zen Buddhists and I can assure you that tower is not stable.'

At that moment, further pieces of glass and masonry

dripped off the tower. 'See,' she said. 'Man's intellect could not create such a building without pieces falling off.'

A loud disagreement broke out between different people, and it looked as if a fistfight might start. Jed and Melanie hung back with their group who were consulting their Way manuals.

'Look. I've found something here,' Jan said, her face aglow. *"The wise ones who had it all figured out will be exposed as fools. The smart people who thought they knew everything will turn out to know nothing."*

Those around her all laughed.

'I love the Way manual,' Tim said. 'It never lets you down.'

They all dodged around the arguing group, and checking their compasses, they found the direction Home veered away from the tower. A wide road turned towards the university, and many chose that path, but their narrower path climbed out of a valley, and into open country. They walked on in silence.

Jed studied Tim as they walked. He reminded him of his father, and the memories were not happy ones. Jed wondered how his mum and Isla were getting on without him. His dad could rot in hell for all he cared.

19 PREPARING FOR THE MOUNTAINS

The campfire blazed brightly as the group sat around, warming themselves and chatting. Geoff and Jed were discussing football.

'Who do you support then, Jed?' Geoff asked in his broad Yorkshire accent.

'Spurs.'

'Oh aye.'

'What about you?'

'Leeds.'

'Really. Not done much have they?'

Geoff gave him the 'what do the young know' look. 'Under Don Revie, we won the First Division twice and Leeds was the last winners of the First Division.'

'First Division? Long time ago, then.'

'Not so long ago that I don't remember it, young Jed.' He gave him a playful nudge.

Tim looked up from his Way manual that he had been reading. 'I think we need to prepare ourselves. I've been reading the manual and looking at where the Way appears to be taking us.' He glanced up, and pointed to the high, snow-covered peaks that loomed before them. 'We're going to have to cross those. It's going to be quite a slog.'

'Isn't there another path?' Jed asked. 'Surely Yeshua wouldn't put us in danger? I mean I've done no mountaineering.'

'We might die of exposure or fall off or get lost,' said Jan. 'I'm not sure I could climb over the mountains.' She shook her head. 'Those days are long gone.'

Tim smiled at Jan. 'I was reading about one of the Way walkers who struggled to fulfil what Yeshua had called him to. He wrote, *"I can do all things through him who strengthens me."* He never said it was going to be easy.'

Jed grinned. 'Yeshua told me that when I had to cross the chasm.'

The others smiled at Jed.

Jan's bottom lip trembled and her voice wavered. 'I'll try.'

Tim stood up and stretched. 'Tomorrow morning, before we set off, we must check we have enough food, firewood and warm clothes. We need to be ready. There may be one or two last farms we can buy provisions before we are out beyond civilisation.'

'I shall need hiking clothes. A sari is not suitable for climbing those mountains,' Sahila said.

They all rose early, packed up their tents, and spent a little time checking they had enough supplies. Between them, it seemed they had warm clothes, but there was a shortage of gloves, hats and thick socks. The weather had been too pleasant to need them recently.

'Although I'm keen to get on continue our journey, we must have enough warm clothes and food. I think we should go back to that last town, and buy what we need,' Tim said.

They started returning the way they had come. Almost immediately they met a group walking the opposite direction. 'You're going the wrong way,' a teenager wearing a T-shirt, shorts and flip-flops said. They were all dressed more for a day at the beach, than to cross snowy mountains.

'We know. We're getting some more warm clothes. We have to cross those mountains,' Tim said as he pointed to the distant peaks. 'You might like to get a bit of warmer gear too.'

'Nah, we're fine. We're young and healthy. We can

manage, thanks.'

The group of young people ran off down the road, kicking a football, and laughing about the mountains up ahead.

A little further on, an elderly man stood by the road, dressed in tatty clothing, but with an enormous billboard round his neck declaring SALE. A mangy dog lay beside him. In a tired voice, the man was calling out, 'Sale. Sale this way. Everything necessary for the mountains, this way.' He pointed towards a path which wound down into a valley towards a warehouse in the distance.

'Just what we need,' Jed said and everyone, apart from Tim, agreed, and seemed delighted they would not have to go all the way back to the town to buy the things they needed.

'I'm not sure I'm happy about this,' Tim said, frowning. 'Yeshua loves to provide for his children, but something about this is not right.'

The rest of the group though were eager to get to the warehouse, make their purchases, and get going. Melanie looked at the forlorn dog and leaned down to stroke him. Fleas jumped off the dog onto her hand, eager for fresh blood.

'Ugh,' she said, flicking all the fleas away. The dog's miserable eyes peered back at her as if to say, 'don't believe him.' He started to scratch, and Melanie stepped back with a questioning look, but he just gazed back at her with his hangdog eyes.

They set off down the path hurrying towards the warehouse. No matter how quickly they ran, it never seemed to get any closer.

'This is weird,' Jed said. 'How come we're not getting any nearer?'

He stopped to look at the warehouse, and as he peered at it, he noticed for the first time it was actually a burnt-out shell. He ran to catch up with the others to tell them, but as he did so, his knees sank into a boggy marsh that everyone had walked into unawares. They all tried to turn around, but the watery ground seemed to suck them in. A foul-smelling odour rose from the disturbed marsh.

'Ugh. That stinks,' Jed said.

Cries of dismay rang out around him as everyone struggled back through the foul-smelling swamp that slurped and drew them down. Jed was one of the first to pull himself out and he flopped down away from the marsh to catch his breath.

'Jed. Come and help the others,' Tim said.

Jed pretended not to hear.

Tim came over and pulled Jed to his feet. 'Come and

help the others.'

Jed glared at him with a mutinous expression, before stumbling over, and helping pull the others from the evil smelling bog.

As soon as the last person was back on solid ground, Jed scowled at Tim, and went and plonked himself down next to Melanie with his back away to the group. 'I hate Tim.'

Melanie frowned. 'Maybe he's not too keen on you either.'

'We should find another group.'

'I like this one. They're safe.'

Jed stared into the distance, a stubborn look on his face. Melanie and Tim exchanged raised eyebrows.

When everyone had caught their breath, they pulled themselves up covered in the foul stinking mud, and re-traced their steps back to the Way.

The old man and his dog had disappeared, but they sat down, and used water from their bottles to clean themselves up a bit. 'Come on,' said Tim. 'We may have time to get to the town tonight, buy our provisions, clean up, and get on our way.'

That night at the campsite, they sat around, faces miserable, shoulders slumped, and hardly speaking to one another. It had been too dark to go shopping when they arrived, and all they had managed was food and a shower. Tim sat reading his Way manual. 'I knew I should have read it first. There are no shortcuts to walking Yeshua's way. Listen to this, *"The wisdom of the wise keeps life on track; the foolishness of fools lands them in the ditch,"* or the marsh.'

Other travellers they met had been either sympathetic, or laughed. 'Fell for that old man and his dog routine. Too good to be true is because it is.'

'We've lost two days now. Tomorrow we will shop, and wash our clothes, and make sure we're ready for the mountains. Now. Get a good night's sleep.'

Jed and Melanie climbed into their tents. Jed soon fell asleep, but spent the night dreaming of evil smelling bogs, and an old man and his dog laughing at them.

20 THE MOUNTAINS

It took a whole day before they were clean, their clothes washed, and they had plenty of warm clothes and other provisions.

The mood of the group was a little subdued after wasting time listening to the battered old man and his mangy dog. They passed him in the same spot, and a few of them argued with him about what he was doing.

'Just doing my job,' the old man muttered.

They were able to warn another group, walking in the opposite direction, but making their way towards him. 'Don't listen to the old man and his dog, whatever you do. There's no shop, no sale, but a bog.'

'Thanks. We don't need anything, anyway, now.'

'Why not?'

'Those mountains are tough; too high and very icy. We turned back. We'll find a different path.'

'The Way manual says there is no other path.'

'The Way manual doesn't know everything. We'll find something else, don't worry.'

Tim looked at them with a sad expression on his face. 'Good luck.' His voice though made clear he thought they were going to need every bit of luck they could find.

The Way climbed higher and higher into the mountains. At first, the path was very attractive winding along steep rocky valleys, fir trees clinging to the slopes and wild flowers tucked into every crevice. Ice-cold rivers bubbled and gurgled down the rocky riverbed. Occasionally, the path crossed pasture covered in grass that was sparse but splattered with multi-coloured alpine flowers. Sheep and goats were grazing on the pasture with an occasional goatherd.

Gradually though the path began to peter out. It became increasingly difficult to find.

'This isn't right.' Tim stopped, and the group gathered around him. 'The Way may be narrow, but it never disappears.'

Everyone looked around as if to find an alternative, but there was no sign of a proper Way. Ian climbed up the mountain slope to see if he could discover the Way, but shaking his head, he re-joined the others.

'Did anyone notice that narrow path going off on the left when we set out this morning?' Jan asked. 'I wondered about it, but I was so focused on keeping my feet, and not slipping that I didn't really bother about it.'

'I saw it, but it looked really unlikely,' Melanie said.

A few others had also seen it.

Tim sighed deeply. 'Com'on. Back we go. Again.'

Shoulders slumped, everyone turned around, and trudged back the way they had come.

Suddenly, Geoff slipped and started to slide down the mountain on his back. 'Help!'

He bounced and rolled down the slope before coming to rest against a boulder, but his white face, and trembling hands showed how shaken he was.

'Help him, Jed,' Tim said.

'Why me?'

'Because you're the youngest and fittest.'

Jed glared at him. 'Ian's the strongest.'

They stood glowering at one another, till Jed turned and carefully picked his way down to Geoff. He helped him to his feet, and together they scrambled back up the slope.

'Concentrate, please. It's still a dangerous path we're

on,' Tim said. 'Well done, Jed,' he added as an afterthought.

Jed kicked a stone, and his lip curled before turning away from Tim.

The group continued their slow progress back down the mountain. After several hours, they were almost back to their last campsite, when they saw a narrow, rocky path heading off down into a valley.

'Is this it, Jan?' Tim asked.

'Yes, I think so. Not very promising.'

'We'll try this and see where it goes. Let's stop and have some food. We still have a couple of hours before it's dark.'

As they turned down the path, they spotted a blood tipped pole about five metres from the turning. 'I missed that,' Tim said. The path led them down into a steep-sided, rocky gorge with trees clinging onto the rock face on both sides. The views were spectacular, but the group could not admire them as it took all their concentration to keep on the track, and not slip and plunge into the gorge. It was becoming darker and darker because of the sun setting, but also because they seemed to be climbing lower and lower beneath the mountains.

'One torch between two.' Tim's voice rang out from

the front. 'Cave entrance coming up.'

They all stopped, and dug into their backpack pockets for a torch, both hand held and head mounted ones. At the entrance to the cave, they turned around, and in what was left of the light, they peered back up the trail to see where they had come.

'It's so steep. Amazing we made it safely,' Melanie said to Jed.

'Yeah. What's next d'you think?'

Melanie shrugged. 'Are you okay, Jed? Your limp seems bad today.'

'I'm alright. Cold doesn't help, and neither does he.' Jed nodded at Tim.

'We'll get inside the cave out of the cold, set up camp and make fires,' Tim said.

The floor in the cave was bumpy and stony, but they managed to clear spaces to lay out the sleeping bags, and with campfires burning brightly, they could eat before settling down for sleep.

21 GRANDFATHER HEMAN

Jed prised his eyes open and saw dim daylight infiltrating the cave. It felt odd to wake up in the dark like a winter's morning at home. The others were yawning and stretching, and before long someone had lit a brightly burning fire, while Jan made coffee and tea, and Ian passed bread and jam round.

'It is vital we keep together on this path. We must be lit by at least two torches at all times so we don't lose the Way. I read in my Way manual today about the old road. This looks like it. Maybe yesterday we should have asked for directions to save ourselves from wasting all that time. Let's ask Yeshua today to keep us on the tried-and-true road.'

Everyone raised their voices to Yeshua to guide them and look after them as they took this Way under the mountains.

'This is scary,' Jed whispered to Melanie. 'I'm not sure I like the idea of walking in the dark for ages.'

'No alternative really, is there?' Melanie grinned at Jed. 'Piece of cake compared to dragging you out of the gaming rooms.'

Jed smiled wanly, but shouldered his backpack, and together they set off down a path that led away from the familiar world of sunshine, rain, snow, landscapes, cities, towns and villages to walk the Way into the unknown dark world.

For the first few hours, the track ran along tunnels, across caves, and they even had to navigate a few potholes, where the sunlight filtered from above, climbing to find another tunnel a few metres up the rock face. Often, the ascent was slippery with rainwater pouring over the rock walls.

If the Way was not obvious, poles dipped in blood marked the path, the tops shimmering red in the glow of their torches.

As they crossed yet another cave, this one with a large lake in the centre, they kept hearing scuffling sounds.

'Is that rats?' Melanie asked.

'Dunno,' Jed said. 'I've been hearing odd noises for hours.'

'I keep hearing those sounds too,' Jan said her eyes gleaming frightened in the torchlight.

'Let's stop for something to eat and drink,' Tim said. 'Maybe we'll be able to see what it is.'

The sandy beach surrounding the lake was quite comfortable to sit on as they chomped on sandwiches and fruit, gazing at the flat surface of the lake shimmering eerily in the torchlight. The odd noises, which had stopped, suddenly started again, and they projected an enormous shadow of a man onto the ceiling from the light of their torches.

Jan screamed. 'Do you see that? There are monsters down here.'

A slightly mocking laugh echoed round the cave. 'Monsters, hey? I don't think so.' A short, clean-shaven man stepped into the light followed by about 10 men, women and children. They carried three lanterns on poles that cast a shadowy pall. The man stood a little over a metre tall, but perfectly proportioned. He wore jeans with braces over a checked shirt, and a large straw hat. Each of the rest of the group was the same height, the men similarly dressed, and the women wearing dresses and headscarves. All of them had sturdy shoes on their feet.

The leader of the group bowed slightly to Tim. 'Welcome to our world. We are Yeshua's Ministers of the Mountains. Few people make it this far. Most turn back before they reach here.' The man spoke in precise, clipped tones.

Melanie however was captivated by another feature of these unusual people. She whispered to Jed. 'Their eyes!'

'Yeah. They're huge and look at the pupils. Must be to help them see in the dark,' he whispered back.

Their leader glared at Melanie and Jed. 'Yeshua placed us here to render assistance to any Way walkers, and to rescue any that are daft enough to get themselves into a precarious predicament.'

'A what?' Jed asked.

'Danger or a stupid place.' The man scowled at Jed afresh, as if he were daft enough to get himself into a precarious predicament.

Jed raised his eyebrows and looked down to stop himself from laughing. The man might be short, yet he reminded Jed of his headteacher, very serious looking with his huge eyes and his old-fashioned way of talking.

Tim stepped forward. 'Thank you, sir,' he said, holding out his hand. The leader shook it.

'Do you have a name?'

'Of course, Grandfather Heman.'

'Sir. Do you have any advice for the onward journey?'

"Commit thy way unto the King; trust also in him; and he shall bring it to pass." the leader said in a very earnest voice, like a judge passing sentence.

'Thank you, sir,' Tim said.

'We found one of yours,' a high-pitched voice suddenly said. 'He was lost down here.'

'Quiet now, young Hezekiah,' Grandfather Heman said, turning to his group. 'Leave this to your elders and betters.'

Young Hezekiah, who had rushed forward full of enthusiasm, turned around and slunk pack to join the rest of them. A lady wearing a little headscarf and apron clipped him round the ear. 'Behave.'

'Yes, Mother.'

'We do indeed have a young 'un of yours. Found wandering in the dark, no light, no proper clothes and very frightened, I think,' Grandfather Heman said. 'Come along.'

The group followed him into a side tunnel that opened up into a small cave in which sat one of the teenagers that they had met on the Way earlier. He was shivering and looked so dejected.

'Hello. Am I glad to see you. I thought I was going to be stuck here forever.'

'Hello. What's your name?' Tim asked, running his hand through his hair.

'Brad.'

'What happened?'

'After we met you, we all ran up the path into the mountains. Things started to go wrong fairly soon. We had not properly equipped ourselves for the mountains. Did you know the path ran out?'

Tim nodded.

'I was really unhappy about continuing. So me and another lad turned around to try that other path that I expect you used.'

They all nodded.

'We found the cave entrance, but after a short way into the dark, Tom decided he had had enough, so he turned back.'

Jan had dug into her backpack and wrapped Brad in an aluminium blanket.

'I was certain this was the Way, but my torch ran out of power. I didn't have any warm clothes, and hardly any food. I became lost.' His voice quivered. 'These people found me and they had some food, but not much else. Fortunately, you turned up soon afterwards.'

'Foolish young man,' Grandfather Heman said, peering at him. 'Fortunate that Yeshua sent us, and these good folks to help you.'

'Why didn't you turn around, and get food, clothes and equipment before entering the cave?' Tim asked.

'Seemed like too much hard work. I was confident we could manage. Big mistake.'

'Trust in Yeshua and not yourself, young man.' Grandfather Heman said, before turning to the lady. 'I hope you are noting the folly of youth, Muriel.'

'Yes, sir,' she bobbed a curtsey, and gave young Hezekiah another clip to show she had understood.

By this time, everyone had opened their backpacks, and was pulling out warmer clothes and shoes for Brad. 'Is it alright if we light a fire?' Tim asked.

'Yes, sir. It is.'

'I think we may stay here to rest and then get going again in a few hours.'

Grandfather Heman nodded. 'We will leave you, then but one last piece of advice. Beware the bats. Their bite is fearsome.'

'Where are they, and how do we fight them?' Tim asked.

'You can't. They come, without warning, out of the dark, so always have a light on. If attacked use your torches and Way manuals. If your open them, and read the words of truth, they will shine brightly. The bats hate the light.'

The group all looked at one another with fearful eyes.

'May Yeshua bless your journey and lead you to the City of Light.'

Tim bowed to Grandfather Heman, and before they knew it, the party had disappeared into the darkness, the noise of their scuffling all that was left of them.

22 THE BATS

It was impossible to tell whether it was night or day, so after a few hours' rest, the group packed up, ate a hurried breakfast, and continued following the Way.

They soon arrived at an enormous cavern, covered in stalagmites pushing up from the floor, and stalactites clinging from the ceiling. Their shapes were remarkable, some looking like a bird on a perch, or an old woman hunched over, and as the group wound around them, following the Way marker poles, they stopped to point out and stare at the incredible display that shimmered in the torchlight.

'This cave is huge,' Jan said shining her torch up to the ceiling, and into the far reaches of the cavern. 'How many thousands of years did it take to form all these stalagmites and stalactites?'

'What's that?' Jed asked, staring up at the roof.

'Where?' Jan played the torchlight on the stalactites.

'There.' Jed pointed up, as small shapes flitted in and out of the columns of limestone.

'Yeah. There's more.' Melanie's torch flicked around

at several more shapes.

'They must be the bats. Let's hurry,' Tim said, making off for the far side of the cave.

High-pitched squeaks mingled with the constant drip dripping of water that echoed round the vast cavern. Jed's stomach churned as he remembered an occasion when his granddad had taken him on a night hike as a treat. Jed had never liked the dark as a child, and when bats started wheeling and whirling around them so close that he felt their wings brush his face, he had squealed like a captured pig. His granddad had laughed, and tried to reassure him, but Jed was so freaked, he ran shrieking back down the path, flapping at imaginary bats.

'Quick!' Jan's voice was anxious as she ran, hopping over and around the stalagmites.

At the far end of the cavern, a tunnel led out into the blackness. They scurried for the dark opening.

'That was close,' Tim said, as he hovered at the tunnel entrance, making sure everyone had escaped from the cave.

The tunnel was short, and led down a rocky slope into another cave that was smaller, but also dripping with water. They walked across the cavern, recovering their breath, but before they were halfway across, the most terrifying flurry of squeaking and zooming shapes attacked them.

'Bats.' They all cried out and took evasive action. Some curled into a tight ball whilst frantically digging into their backpacks for torches and Way manuals. Those who already had their torches out tried to pinpoint a bat in the beam. It was difficult, and everyone had to be alert to duck and swerve to avoid the diving bats.

Jed ran, and crouched down in a corner, eyes tight shut and hands over his ears, every shred of bravery disappearing in craven cowardice. The screeches from the bats reminded Jed of the terrible whine of falling doodlebug bombs from the Second World War that he had seen in a film.

At that moment. Melanie cried out, 'Jed. I've been bitten. It's so painful.' She clasped her arm and dropped to the floor. 'Jed, please help.' Melanie's piteous cry, so unlike her normal forthright manner, touched Jed's heart. His friend needed him. He'd always depended on her, but now she was in trouble.

'I can't,' he whispered. 'I just can't.' He clasped his hands even tighter over his ears.

'Jed.' Again, her cry reached out to him.

Jed looked up from his hiding place. Fear gripped him with a terrible churning in his stomach. Everything within him wanted to hide until someone else dealt with the situation. He was shivering uncontrollably, but suddenly something inside him snapped. He grabbed hold of his torch and Way manual, stood up, and then rushed over to defend Melanie. 'Right. Let's sort these bats.'

All his anger, frustration and rage at his father's betrayal, and his granddad's death focused on trying to rescue his friend who had saved him. He swiped at every incoming bombardment, occasionally making contact. One cluster of bats appeared to be gathering to focus their attack on Melanie and Jed. They hovered overhead just long enough for Jed to see in his torchlight their snout like noses, big black eyes, huge furry ears and leathery wings.

As if in battle formation, they dived towards Jed, standing over Melanie. With a loud, adrenaline fuelled cry that overcame his fear, Jed shone his torch on bat after bat. At first his aim was wild, and too short to be effective, but as he ducked and veered away from bat after bat, he quickly learned that he needed to keep the beam of the torch on a bat for a few seconds, following its dive till it went into a fatal tailspin, and burst into flames on contact with the ground.

Jed became angrier and angrier, yelling, and pinpointing one bat after another as he twisted and turned, leaping to one side and then the next, avoiding every attack but protecting Melanie who was curled up tight in a ball, sobbing. He even made contact with his fist on one animal, which bit his hand. It stung terribly, and Jed had to keep flipping it to stop the pain from paralysing his arm.

His open Way manual also proved an effective weapon as he heard Tim declaring words from the book. *I am the light of the world.* The words lifted off Jed's Way manual, formed an arrow, and flew at a bat, piercing its body, and causing it to crash and burn.

Time and again the bats attacked, not only Jed and Melanie, but the rest of the group who also were quickly learning the best ways to defeat them. However, as the bats were downed, the decreasing number of them focused their attack afresh on Melanie, and Jed was becoming more and more aggressive in his assaults on them. His battle cries grew louder and louder, and he even managed to strike one or two bats with his Way manual, flooring them.

One or two of the others wanted to come to his assistance, but Tim held them back. 'This is Jed's battle.' In a whisper he added, 'with himself.'

After what felt like an eternity, but was probably merely a few minutes, the endless stream of bats dwindled, and those left gave up their attack.

Jed stood panting heavily, his hands on his knees, white faced, shaking from shock and exertion, and with tears streaming down his face. Melanie uncurled, looking with surprise and amazement, though her face was creased in pain from her bat bite.

Tim strode over, and took Jed in his arms, and held him in a tight embrace till the sobbing died into a few hiccoughs. 'Well done, my boy. That took guts.'

Jed's last few sobs turned into deep breaths. Melanie pulled herself to her feet, cradling her injured arm, but with a huge grin on her face. She held out a knuckle to Jed, and they touched fists. 'Didn't know you had it in you.'

Jed smiled weakly. 'Neither did I.'

Tim led them all away from the main cave to a smaller cavern with a low ceiling, where they all collapsed, and took out water bottles.

'I'm shattered,' Jed said.

'We'll find somewhere safer to camp, eat and sleep. Not here, and not out there, in case they come back,' Tim said.

When everyone had taken a drink and had applied healing balm to bat bites and other injuries sustained during the attack, Tim led them back to the bat cave to rejoin the Way. They hurried along the wall, gazing fearfully at the ceiling, but all they heard were a few squeaks, but no bats were to be seen.

Tim guided them down through a variety of long tunnels, some with high roofs, and others so low they had to crawl on hands and knees, but whenever the path was in doubt, there would be a blood-tipped pole.

After an hour, everyone was begging Tim to find somewhere to stop and rest.

'I'm exhausted,' Jan said. 'I don't know if I can keep going.'

'Me too.' Melanie's eyes were white in the darkness. 'That bat bite has drained me of all energy.'

Jed was stumbling along behind the group, dragging himself through the low tunnels, till he collapsed on the floor. 'I'm not sure I can go on.'

Tim squeezed past the others to kneel by Jed. 'I really need you to dig deep and keep going. We can't stop here.' He took hold of Jed's hands and squeezed them, pulling Jed upright. 'Remember, "*I can do all things through Yeshua who gives me strength*"'.

'Okay. I'll try.'

For another half hour, they plodded on in silence. No one had the energy to talk. Finally, the tunnel opened out into a cave with a river flowing through it. The banks of the river were rocky, but away from the water, along the sides of the cave were some flatter rocks covered in a thin layer of sand. Everyone dropped their backpacks there, and lay on the floor, puffing and groaning.

'Don't fall asleep yet. Make camp. Get your sleeping bag out and I'm certain there will be a Wayfarer bar in your backpack,' Tim said. 'Geoff, help me make a fire so we have light to see, and save our torch batteries. Then we can make a hot drink.'

Everyone pulled out their sleeping bag and discovered a Wayfarer bar. Sitting on their sleeping bag, and leaning against their backpacks, they happily munched, watching Tim and Geoff make the fire.

'That's better,' said Jan, as she threw the purple wrapper of her Wayfarer bar into the flames. 'I'm not just feeling fuller, but also restored, not so heavy-hearted.'

'Even the pain in my arm from the bat bite is easing,' Melanie said. 'I feel better too.'

'I'm still shattered,' Jed said. 'I'm going to sleep.'

'Well done again, Jed. Sleep well.' Tim came over and gave him a hug. In his ear, he whispered. 'You served Yeshua well.'

Jed returned the hug and snuggled into his sleeping bag.

23 FORGIVENESS

His eyes had hardly closed before Jed found himself standing in a street, and outside a house that was instantly recognisable to him. It was his street and his house.

He had lived here all his life. He knew every other house on this road, and who lived there. Old Mr and Mrs Peter's bungalow with its immaculate front garden, spotless porch and front door and pristine interior. When he had been younger, they had always given him a small gift on his birthday and at Christmas, but as he grew older and surlier, ignoring them, the gifts and the greetings stopped. Isla continued to be fussed over.

There was the chaotic front garden and house of the Harrisons, where twins two years younger than himself lived. Next door the collapsing wall and overgrown garden of the Butchers, and across the road, the block paved anonymity of the newcomers with their flash Audi SUV gracing the hard standing of what used to be a front garden. He knew them all.

As he stood outside his house, he saw his mum's car pull up, and a younger version of himself jump out of the car before it had hardly stopped, and rush up, and lean on the front doorbell. 'Dad! Dad!' he heard himself yell. 'Look what I got for my birthday.'

He recognised the day immediately. It had been his 11th birthday. No one answered the door. His mother with Isla in her arms, and two bags hanging from her shoulders staggered to the front door before placing her burdens on the ground, and fishing out her key, and opening the door.

Jed had pushed past her, his birthday present proudly in his hands, and rushed into every room downstairs, continuing to shout for his dad. Determined to find him, he bounded up the stairs, running in and out of every bedroom and bathroom, until he stood panting on the landing at the top of the stairs.

'He's not here.' His voice was full of disappointment.

At the bottom of the stairs, his mum stood with a piece of paper in her trembling hands. Tears dripped down her cheeks. She ignored Isla, standing bawling at her knees, demanding to be picked up. 'He's gone,' she said.

'Gone,' Jed had said. 'Where? To the pub? Granny and Grandad's?'

'No. Gone for good gone.'

Jed dropped his new birthday present at the top of

the stairs and stumbled down them. 'I don't get it. What do you mean?' he wailed; his face white. 'He can't have gone.'

His mother used a vulgar word, something Jed had never heard in his life before. 'Well, he has. Off with his other woman.'

'He's got someone else?' With no further words, Jed stamped back up the stairs, picked up his birthday present, slammed into his bedroom, and banged the door shut.

Out of his mouth exploded every terrible word he had ever heard in his life. The older Jed watched as his younger self started to throw things around his room, cursing and swearing. His mother ran up the stairs leaving Isla weeping downstairs and burst into the room.

'Jed. Stop it. Stop it.' She hauled him into her arms and held him firmly until the dreadful rage started to pass.

'Why? Doesn't he love us anymore?' Jed took deep tremulous gulps.

'Things haven't been quite right between us for a little while, love.' His mother smoothed his hair, and gently patted his back. 'I thought there was someone else, but I never thought he'd do this.' Anger came back into her voice. 'I need to phone Nan.'

She looked into his eyes to check he had calmed down. He nodded and drooped down the stairs behind her. She picked up Isla, and soothed her, before pulling her phone out of her bag, and calling her mother.

Ten minutes later Nan arrived. She took Isla, and bathed her, and put her to bed, all the time talking quietly to either his mum or Jed. 'I'm sorry, Jed. On your birthday, too. Did you have a good time?'

He nodded, and tears started to drip down his face. 'The lads clubbed together and bought me that new racing game.' He took a deep breath. 'I was going to play it with dad.' He started to sob again.

Nan took him into her arms. 'You'll have to try teaching it to granddad.'

Jed smiled weakly at her. 'No thanks. I'll get Ali and Tom round.'

Nan smiled. 'Good idea.'

Jed stood outside his house, remembering how over the next few weeks, something withered inside him. He withdrew into himself. His granddad had done everything he could to soothe Jed's battered feelings, but when he had suddenly died only three months later, Jed took a step into the darkness of self-pity and black disillusionment and despair. He became angry with everyone, even his friends. Gradually they backed off, tired of being the butt of his resentment.

One evening, his dad had come round to collect his things, and had tried to explain to Jed what had happened. Jed recalled, as he watched him now, how bitter and offended he had felt. How all he could think about was himself; how hurt he had been, how hurt and angry he still was. He actually started to blush as he remembered his selfishness, and his refusal to even consider how anyone else was feeling.

At that moment, his granddad stood beside him. He placed his hand around Jed's shoulders and squeezed. 'It's time to forgive.'

'I can't,' Jed said.

'You must. You'll never be free otherwise.'

'But he dumped us. He walked out. He just left us.'

'I know, but as Yeshua has forgiven you, so you must forgive him.'

Jed turned to his granddad. 'Why did you have to die? I don't think I'll ever get over that.'

'You will but not until you forgive.' He took Jed's chin in his hand and looked with such love and acceptance into his eyes that Jed's resolve to hang onto his grievances, no matter who he hurt, melted.

A vision of Yeshua on the cross, dying in agony, and

then urging him across the chasm thawed his cold, hard heart.

'How?'

Granddad stepped back. 'Say it aloud. Speak out your heart and be free.'

For what seemed ages, Jed poured out his anger, his bitterness and his forgiveness to his dad for abandoning him and neglecting him. Granddad stood, tears in his eyes listening to Jed. 'And I'm sorry for blaming everyone for your death.' He smiled through trembling lips, then continued. 'I'm so sorry for being selfish and not looking out for my mum and being a horrible brother to Isla.' Jed took another wavering breath. 'And for being a right punk to my grandparents and my schoolmates.'

Jed looked upwards and puffed out his cheeks. 'Is that it?'

'For the moment.' Granddad embraced him. 'Receive Yeshua's forgiveness and his freedom.'

Jed gazed at him and exhaled a long breath. 'I do feel better. It's like a great weight has gone. No, it's more like the hard lump inside.' He patted his chest and grinned. 'It's melted. What next?'

'Home,' Granddad said. 'I'll be waiting.'

24 HORATIO AND MOLLIE

The sound of singing woke everyone up. It was a very mournful song and though the tune seemed familiar, especially to the older ones in the group, the words were all wrong.

Dark river

Flowing to the light

Time to seek the sun again.

Arise, shine, come out of the night

And walk in the light of day.

Jed and Melanie, along with the rest of the group prised their eyes open, yawning expansively. People scratched their heads, and stretched as they sat up, and tried to see in the darkness who or what was singing.

Tim and Ian played their torch's beam on the water, and gasping, shook their heads in amazement. A large punt with an upturned bow, looking remarkably similar to a Venetian gondola glided up the river towards them.

On a wooden platform towards the stern, a man stood dressed in a blue striped t-shirt, black trousers with a red sash, and a large straw boater on his head. He had an extravagant moustache that hung over his lips giving him a lugubrious expression. He manoeuvred the craft using a long pole.

At the bow stood a lady similarly dressed in a red striped t-shirt, black trousers and large straw boater. Her grey hair hung in a single plait down her back, but her face looked far younger than the grey hair would suggest. She was guiding the vessel with hand signals as she sang.

Melanie and Jed stood up and watched as the man punted the boat with great skill through the water to a stone wharf, where the lady jumped off, and quickly tied the boat up to a ring on the wall.

'Good morning, Way walkers,' the man said, coming over to them. 'Your transport to the outside world awaits.' His voice sounded very gloomy.

The woman, on the other hand, having tied up the boat, strode across to the group. 'Come on. Get the kettle on. Time for a cuppa before we go.'

Jan laughed, and handed the kettle to Jed to fill, as Tim and Geoff blew on the embers of last night's fire and placed a little of their dwindling wood supply on the flames.

'How did you know to come and find us?' Melanie asked.

'Grandfather Heman told us you were on the way.'

The man held out his hand to Tim. 'I'm Horatio and this is Molly. We have been situated here by Yeshua to transport Way walkers out of the caves.'

'I'm so pleased,' Sahila said, as she toasted bread on a long-handled fork over the flames whilst making sure Melanie did not burn the scrambled egg she was stirring. The kettle boiled, and Jan made tea for everyone.

'Did you manage to avoid the bats?' Molly asked.

'No,' Geoff said. 'We put up a good fight, and young Jed here rose to the occasion.'

Jed blushed and looked down as Geoff punched him lightly on the arm.

'The bats enjoy tormenting Way walkers,' Horatio said, in a miserable voice.

'Why?' Melanie frowned.

'They hate Yeshua, and they can't hurt him, but they can persecute his followers, and try to get them to turn back.' He sighed such a soulful sound.

'But Yeshua turns all these things to the good,' Molly laughed. 'He said, *"How enriched you are when you bear the wounds of being persecuted for doing what is right! For that is when you experience the realm of heaven's kingdom."*

Jed wrinkled his nose. 'That doesn't make any sense. How can you be enriched by being persecuted?'

'Because that is what happened to Yeshua. Way walkers follow in his footsteps,' Tim said, helping to clear up. 'Time to go, I think. I shall be pleased to see the sun and feel fresh air on my face again.'

Everyone hurried to pack up and then stood on the edge of the rocky riverbank.

'Is the boat big enough for all eight of us?' Ian asked. 'I mean I'm not exactly regular size.'

Molly laughed. 'I think so. Let's get the ladies on board first.'

Jed rushed forward, and held out a hand to Jan and Sahila, who smiled at his good manners. He tried to do the same for Melanie. She glared at him. 'I can manage. Save your chivalry for the others.'

Jed looked offended, and almost pushed her into the boat. 'Only trying to help.'

The women sat down at the front of the craft.

Tim stepped forward. 'Brad, you next, and then Ian

and Geoff.' The craft wobbled wildly as Ian stepped on board and sat down at the end away from everyone else.

'Alright?' Tim asked Horatio and Molly, who had been keeping the craft steady as everyone climbed on board.

'Oh yes. Stow the backpacks behind me, then you and the young 'un climb on board, and we're ready.'

Jed and Tim stowed the backpacks in the rear of the punt, and stepped on board, sitting down on either side in the centre of the craft.

'And off we go.' Molly pushed away the punt from the wharf and jumped on board. She took up her position in the bow to act as lookout.

At first the current was sluggish, and they drifted along slowly, Horatio steering the boat in the middle of the stream to maintain steady progress.

Almost imperceptibly, the current started to pick up. The punt flew down the treacherous rapids that tumbled with all manner of eddies and boulders to navigate. Molly called out and gave hand signals to help Horatio keep the craft steady. His punt pole dipped in and out of the water, steering the boat round the hazards. Those on board clung onto the sides of the craft, so they wouldn't be pitched into the rapids, their eyes glancing here and there.

After about half an hour, the tunnel started to lighten, though the river grew ever more hazardous. With daylight, it was easier for Molly to see where the current was flowing. However, they all became aware that as the current grew ever more rapid and dangerous, a thunderous noise increased in volume.

The group's eyes grew wide in terror as they realised they were hurtling towards a waterfall. They could see where the river dropped over the edge at the tunnel entrance, and huge spumes of spray hovered over the cascade.

'Help!' Jan yelled, as the punt lurched.

At the last moment, Horatio steered the craft to one side, straightening the punt, and Molly nipped onto the wooden jetty positioned on the side of the rocky walls, and tied the boat front and rear to rings in the wall.

'Now leave the craft, the biggest ones first, but without your backpacks. We'll pass them up in a moment,' she said.

Ian, Geoff and Tim climbed out of the boat, and held out hands to help the rest. The ladies smiled as they grabbed an extended hand, but Brad and Melanie jumped out unaided. Jed was left to pass the backpacks to Ian's waiting hands.

The first thing everyone did was edge along the jetty

out into the sunshine to stand with their faces upturned to the sun, and let its rays warm them.

'I have so missed the sun,' Jan said.

There were murmurs of agreement all round as everyone gazed at their surroundings to see where they had been delivered. To their right the river dropped vertically over a rock face and beautiful rainbows shimmered in the spray. Ahead, more mountains soared into the distance.

'I thought we might be through the mountains, and out onto the plain beyond,' Ian said.

'No chance.' Geoff shook his head, looking very disappointed. 'Still a distance to go yet.'

'I'm not overly keen on the path ahead,' Tim said, as he pointed to the icy peaks. 'It will take determination to get over those.'

'Whoa. I don't fancy that,' Jed said to Melanie.

Melanie shook her head. 'Neither do I, but I don't think we have much choice.'

Horatio and Molly were getting ready to take their punt away. 'We have a little boathouse back up the tunnel. Only a short distance.' Molly said. 'When we're needed, there's a narrow path along the walls we can haul the boat up to the wharf, where we found you. The last stretch we punt.'

'Thanks so much for fetching us,' Tim said, and everyone added their thanks. They all shook hands and waved as their rescuers disappeared.

'Right. Let's go,' Tim said.

Jed shrugged his backpack onto his sore shoulders and eyed the path ahead.

'Hope this is going to be okay,' he said to Melanie. 'It's not like we're mountaineers.'

'I agree.'

Tim turned to set off up the one path that was visible, but not before Jed noticed how anxious he looked. Heads down, the group followed him.

25 THE HIGH PEAKS

For several hours they climbed higher and higher, aligning themselves to Home on their compass whenever the path divided. The air grew cooler and thinner, and their breathing became heavier. Icy patches that clung to the rocks made the path slippery. The snow that had seemed distant was now lying on the slopes around the path.

Everyone pulled warmer clothing out of their backpacks, and as he did so, Jed noticed that his Bag of Rewards was much heavier now. He jangled it and looked inquiringly at Melanie who shrugged.

They stopped for something to eat. 'I'd love a hot drink,' Jan said.

'Me too,' Melanie said.

'A cup of Ceylon tea,' Sahila's eyes glistened.

'We'll have hot food when we make camp later,' Tim said. 'Let's press on and see if we can find somewhere to shelter safely for the night.'

After a couple more hours of steady, uphill plodding,

they came across a cave, set back above the path. They all scrambled up to it, puffing and panting.

'I am very relieved we've made it here before dark,' Tim said, as the huge orange sun sank behind the mountains. 'Ian, let's get a good fire going. Jan and Sahila please sort out the food. Definitely a hot meal. Brad and Jed make sure we have enough water. There was a small waterfall about 100 metres back down the path, and Melanie sort the beds out please.'

Jed and Brad grabbed all the water carriers and hurried back down the path as the last light of the day faded, and it grew dark. They tried to fill the bottles and carriers as quickly as they could, but it was a messy business in the dark.

Howls in the distance grew nearer and nearer, which made them run back to the cave, but they had a strong sense of being pursued. It was hard to tell if the heavy breathing was their own, or another creature following them. They almost fell into the cave, and around the fire that was burning brightly in the entrance, dropping all the water carriers on the floor.

'You alright?' Geoff asked. 'You're as white as sheets.'

'There's things out there,' Jed said, his hands shaking.

'What ghoulies and ghosties and things that go bump in the night?' Ian laughed.

'No joke. Wild animals.' Brad's teeth were chattering.

Ian said, 'You're safe now. Food's almost ready.'

'Good.'

After a delicious meal of spicy lentil and bean stew, full of vegetables, Tim decided to leave the clearing up till morning. 'Let's get a good sleep, but we'll post a guard just to make sure. Whoever is on watch can keep the fire burning.' He turned to Geoff. 'You first. Then Ian, and I'll take the last watch.'

Melanie had laid out sleeping bags at the back of the cave, and everyone settled down to sleep, but the possibility of wild animals sniffing them out unsettled them. Jan and Sahila tossed and turned, Tim was reading his Way manual by torchlight, and everyone else lay listening to Ian's snoring, the only one who seemed able to sleep.

Throughout the dark hours, the sounds of the night, real or imagined, kept most of them from nodding off. It was not until the first cold fingers of dawn seeped into the cave, and the snuffling from outside had subsided, that everyone slept. Tim sat near the fire, throwing the occasional branch of their dwindling supply onto the dying embers.

He lit the camping stove, filled the kettle from the water carriers, and made tea for everyone, waking them gently. Groans and muttered complaints filled the cave, and with much grumbling the group prepared for the day.

That morning, the path became even more treacherous with snow and ice tightly packed onto every surface.

'I am so glad I have my hiking pole.' Jan managed to puff to Sahila, as her feet almost slid out from underneath her. All Sahila could manage was a nod of agreement.

At that moment, Tim stopped. They faced a vast snowfield that stretched up the mountain. Across it, blood tipped poles had been placed at regular intervals, but there were few footprints of anyone that might have gone before.

'Time to rope up,' Tim said. 'I'll go first, then Melanie and Bradley. Geoff in the middle, Jan and Sahila, then Jed and Ian at the back in case any of us fall.'

When they were all roped up, Tim set off, prodding his pole into the snow before every footstep. On more than one occasion, his pole almost disappeared, and they had to try to the right or left to reach the next Way marker. It was slow progress and after an hour, Tim stopped so everyone could catch their breath.

'The thin air is making breathing difficult,' Tim said between gulps of air. 'We're almost through the snowfield, and I'm hoping we will reach the summit before dark.'

No one had any breath for conversation, and they trudged up. Far above them, a bird of prey soared, looking for food. Geoff glanced up to admire the bird, and as he did so, his feet skidded from underneath him, and he started to slide down the snowy slope.

'Jed. Hold fast,' Ian yelled, taking a firm grip on the rope which was wrapped around his shoulder.

Jed dug his feet into the snow, one leg above the other, and grabbed hold of the rope. It was almost yanked out of his gloved hands as Geoff came to an abrupt halt, almost causing Jan and Sahila to fall too, but the rest of the group had snatched the rope above, and it held. They all stood stock still, as if frozen, till Ian said, 'now carefully, Jed and I will pull Geoff back. The rest of you stand still and maintain tension on the rope.'

Geoff scrambled back up the slope till they were all back together. Everyone was white, none more so than Geoff, and the ladies were shivering, and not just from the cold.

'Everyone, take a deep breath. Are we all okay?' Tim asked.

They all nodded, though Jed's hands were shaking

almost uncontrollably. Even Ian looked pale under his brown skin.

'Sorry everyone. I was watching that bird of prey.' Geoff's laugh was nervous.

'Eyes on the path. We don't want any accidents especially this close to the summit,' Tim said. He checked everyone was ready, and they began again their slow journey across the snowfield. Half an hour later, they reached the other side and found somewhere to sit down, perched on an icy ledge.

'I could kill a cup of tea.' Jan smiled. 'Cold water doesn't do it.'

'We really are nearly there. I'd love to get over the summit tonight, but the light is fading.'

Slow step followed slow step. Jed stopped, and took a deep lungful of air, but it still left him panting. He didn't even have the breath to tease Melanie, as she stood, hands on knees, trying to fill her lungs.

The summit was tantalisingly close, but as they reached a small rise, they all groaned, for they could now see that the summit was still about five hundred metres away. Thoughts of reaching the summit vanished as they saw three orange shapes on the snowy slope in the distance.

'Looks like tents,' Tim said. 'Is anyone there or have

they been abandoned?'

They plodded on and when they drew level, they all sank to their knees in front of the first tent door. Tim unzipped it and gasped at what he saw.

'Ian! Here.'

Ian slithered to join him and peered inside. 'Flipping heck.' He turned to look wide-eyed at Tim.

'What?' Everyone else tried to look.

Tim kept them back. 'Someone hasn't made it. I think they're dead.'

'Oh no,' Jan said, her face crumpled.

'I'll check the other tents.' Tim stood, and went to the next tent, unzipped the door. 'Empty'.

He trod with great care to the final tent. 'Two people here. Both dead.' He looked at the rest of the group. 'What a tragedy. They'd almost made it.'

At that moment there was a groan from inside the tent. Jan hurried over, slithering on the ice, and knelt down to ease herself into the tent. 'This one is frozen, but alive,' she said taking hold of a hand, and rubbing it vigorously. 'Can we manage a fire, Tim?'

'I don't think so. The wind will blow it out and we've hardly any fuel left.'

'Geoff. Ian, please help me remove the body to the other tent. What we can do is light the camping stove and try to get some hot drinks and soup going.'

Jan crawled into the tent, as Geoff and Ian moved the body of an older man, still in his sleeping bag, out of the tent, and placed it with the body of an older lady in the first tent.

Melanie's eyes were wide with shock, but following Tim's instruction, she joined Jan, and started to make hot drinks. The water boiled quickly, but the altitude meant it took ages to become hot enough for drinks, and soup made from dried ingredients.

Tim instructed everyone else to erect tents and secure them from the strong and bitterly cold wind.

After a little food, no one was hungry. They settled down, two to a tent, keeping all their clothes on, including their coats, and as many pairs of gloves and socks they had. Jed kept rubbing his feet together to keep the circulation going to try to generate a little warmth.

Jan insisted on staying with the lady who was still alive. All night as the others tried to sleep with the wind howling around them, she kept rubbing the lady's hands and feet, made her a hot water bottle, and shared her clothes and sleeping bag with her.

As the grey of dawn started to lighten the

mountainside, everyone stirred from their dozing. Tim, staying in his tent, took a roll call. When he shouted Jan's name, there was no reply. 'Jan? Jan, are you okay?'

All the response was a weak cry. Tim grabbed his boots, and scrambled across to the tent, and poked his head inside. The elderly lady was sitting, shivering and shaking. 'I'm so sorry. I think she's dead. She gave me her thick jumper, blanket and warm sleeping bag and I think she's frozen to death.'

Tim investigated and found it, as she said.

The lady sobbed, her shoulders shaking. 'We almost made it. We stopped for one last night rather early instead of pressing on. What about the others?'

Tim's face said it all.

'That was my sister and her husband. We've been walking the Way for years, but as we grew older, we dawdled more and more. We ran out of decent equipment.' She took a deep, wavering breath. 'We always wanted to arrive at the City of Light together.' She looked at them with such sadness.

Melanie, who had been shivering outside, squeezed in, and hugged her. 'What's your name?'

'Olive.'

'Jan is in the City of Lights with Yeshua. The Way

manual says *Love one another the way I loved you. This is the very best way to love. Put your life on the line for your friends.* That's what Jan did.' Tim said with a rueful smile.

Later that morning, they took Jan's body, and those of Olive's sister and husband, and placed them on a flat piece of rock, and covered them with stones, creating a cairn. It took most of the morning. Afterwards they stood around the cairn, and remembered Jan and Olive's family, gave thanks for their lives, and thanked Yeshua they were with him.

'We will continue tomorrow. Let's rest and recuperate,' Tim said.

'You'd better have Jan's backpack and equipment,' Melanie said to Olive. 'It doesn't look as if you have any supplies left.'

'Oh I couldn't. I feel awful.'

'You'll feel a lot worse if you get cold and die,' Melanie said.

Jed nudged her. 'Bit harsh.'

Melanie shrugged. 'Go on. Take it,' she said, with a gentle smile.

Olive lifted the backpack as if it might bite her, but as she put on Jan's boots, her face brightened. 'I haven't been warm for days except last night. My boots wore out a little while ago, and I never bothered to replace them. I thought we'd get to the City of Light first.'

Melanie squeezed her shoulder. 'Come on. Let's help get food.'

After supper of beans and stew, made from rehydrated ingredients, they crept back into sleeping bags, and without embarrassment snuggled up together to make sure everyone kept warm. 'Hopefully, this will be our last night on the mountain,' Tim called out. 'Try to get a bit of rest.'

26 OFF THE MOUNTAIN

At first light, they packed up the camp, shivering in the intense cold. Snowflakes drifted around them, and Tim looked up with anxious eyes at the distant sky, where dark grey clouds were gathering.

'We need to hurry. We must be over the summit before that storm arrives,' he said.

The party roped up, and set off, and though they all tried to hurry, the thin air and the effect of altitude slowed them to a snail's pace. Heads down they plodded on. Even Ian the rock, was struggling. Jed's limp becoming more and more pronounced in the cold, but the summit never seemed to get nearer.

'Will we ever get there?' Jed asked, taking great gulps of breath.

'Keep going,' Tim said. 'Help Olive if you can.'

Despite struggling themselves, Melanie and Jed took an arm on each side of her and helped her up the relentless slope.

'Summit.' Tim's voice rang out over the mountain,

and all the rest tried to hurry the last few metres. Standing on the top gasping, they stood to admire the view. Looking back, the way they had come they shook their heads in amazement.

'Look at the town where we bought supplies. It's minute.' Geoff said and chuckled.

'You can even see where Horatio and Molly dropped us off,' Melanie said waving.

'I'm pretty sure they can't see us, Melanie,' Jed said.

'I know but …'

However, the view ahead was breath-taking. The City of Light was now clearly visible. It was vast, resplendent and majestic. Despite the ever-increasing wind that was battering them, they stood with mouths open, gazing at the magnificent scene. High walls surrounded the city that stood on a hill and stretched far beyond where the eye could see. Its tall gates stood open, and people, tiny as ants from this distance, climbed the hill to approach the gates.

'What are those gates made of?' Jed asked.

'I dunno, but they are incredible. In fact, the entire city is amazing.'

'We must move and quickly,' Tim said. 'We cannot stand her gawping, no matter how incredible the view. The wind is gusting stronger and stronger, and I don't want any of us blown off the mountain.'

He set off down the path marked by a blood tipped pole, and everyone followed. As soon as they were off the summit, the wind's strength decreased. The path continued to be treacherous, and Tim soon stopped.

'We must keep roped up.' His face was serious. 'More people fall descending than ascending a mountain. We must concentrate too despite the view.' He glanced briefly at the City of Light.

They slithered on down the slippery track. Nearly everyone skidded at some point, a few landing heavily on their bottoms, and others even sliding down the snowy slopes, but every time the group held the rope firm. Jed rubbed his sore hip more and more, as the cold made it painful.

'I am so glad I'm not on my own, or even just with you, Melanie,' Jed said.

'Told you. Safety in numbers.'

As they descended, so much more quickly than they had ascended, their breathing grew easier and easier. Snow and ice disappeared and though the Way was rocky, and they needed to take great care, their progress was rapid.

The whole mountainside was now bathed in the

magnificent radiance of the City.

They stopped mid-morning, a little distance above the treeline, to eat and they were able to boil water and make hot drinks or soup. Tim stared back up the mountain where the summit had disappeared under dark clouds. 'There's quite a storm raging up there now. Thank Yeshua we were over in time.'

Everyone looked back and shuddered, clutching their hot drinks.

As Olive sipped her soup she said, 'I am very sad to think we were so close and yet my dear husband and sister did not have the joy of completing their course.'

'Does it matter? They're in the City of Light. In fact, why doesn't Yeshua take us straight to the City after we've crossed the chasm,' Jed said.

'The journey is vital to what we do in the City of Light for eternity,' Olive said.

'How?'

'What we learn here, and what we do for Yeshua affects our future life. We must make the most of our journey, and every opportunity he gives to serve him.'

Jed shrugged, and held out his palms, face upward with a look of complete bewilderment.

'How is your Bag of Rewards? Have you looked at it

recently?' Olive asked.

'No, but it feels heavier, and seems to have all sorts of things in it.'

'Yeshua rewards all his loved ones for everything they do in his name, whether showing kindness, saving a life, acts of generosity, anything. You cannot out give him.' She smiled at Jed.

'Once inside the City of Light, the contents of your bag will be thrown into the fire and tested. Those items of lasting value will remain and be rewarded. The rest will be burnt up.'

'Really?' Jed's face was baffled.

'Remember though, you don't do good works to gain a reward, or to impress others. We serve Yeshua because he loves us and made a way across the chasm. You cannot earn any more once you enter the City of Light.'

Jed curled one lip over the other. 'So, you need to do all you can to get loads of rewards before you enter the City.'

'That's right.'

'But what about Jan? Her life was cut short.'

'Ah, but she gave her life saving mine. That is a glorious reward.' Olive looked very sad. 'But my husband and sister died needlessly. They lost many opportunities to add to their rewards.'

Jed looked very thoughtful as Tim encouraged them to prepare to move again. They ambled down the road to a campsite and in no time, tents were up, fires lit and the smell of cooking food made them smile in anticipation.

Later, they disappeared into their tents to sleep better than they had for days.

27 THE CITY GATES

Next morning, the group set out determined to reach the City of Light, but as they drew nearer, their steps slowed as the city's presence overwhelmed them. It dominated the entire landscape. Night and day disappeared as the glory of the city overcame every other light, including the huge, orange sun.

Conversation faltered, and the few words exchanged were done so in whispers. They needed far less food or sleep. Drawing closer to the city constantly energised them. However, what was strange was the villages that clustered round the Way at regular intervals, where travellers could still purchase food and any other supplies that they needed.

'They hardly seem aware of the city,' Melanie said to Jed, gazing at some neighbours laughing and joking amongst themselves.

'I know. You'd think it would fill their lives, being so close. Doesn't make sense.'

'I agree,' Sahila said. 'I can hardly speak for the beauty of the city, yet they laugh and chat as if it is not there.'

'Familiarity. It shields you from the wonder,' Tim said, shaking his head. 'Sad.'

As they reached the slope up to the gates of the City, the group stood and gazed in wonder at the glory radiating from the walls that towered over them. It was quite magnificent.

Jed stopped, his mouth wide open and gazed up at the walls. 'I can't take it all in.'

'I know,' Melanie said. 'What are the walls made of?'

'It's not stone. It's like jewels, but those blocks are huge and polished,' Sahila said.

Geoff stood shaking his head, overawed. 'You can see through those blocks. It might be emerald I suppose. It is green but it's multi-coloured in places and some blocks are blue.'

'The walls can't be breathing, can they?' Olive asked. 'They are just so alive.'

'I don't know, but they're throbbing. You can feel energy pulsing from them.' Geoff said.

They resumed their slow climb to the gates. 'I'm so intimidated. I almost want to turn and run,' Melanie said.

'I know, but I'm drawn like a magnet at the same time,' Jed said.

At the gates, two huge heavenly beings stood, holding mighty scrolls in their hands. They were resplendent, glowing in splendour, robed in white with huge wings on their backs, towering over the group.

'Welcome Way walkers. Approach the gates.'

There was a nervous shuffling forward.

'Who is the least?' one angel asked.

They all looked at one another and then their collective gaze fell on Melanie. Everyone else stepped back.

'What? Not me. I'm the youngest.' Melanie looked round the group. 'Tim should go first. He's led us here.'

The other angel nodded at Tim. 'The first shall be last, and the last first.'

'I agree,' Tim said. 'Melanie has been faithful in all she has done from serving the group to making sure Jed kept to the Way.'

'Approach child.'

Through the gates they could see a pool, glistening in the light, and on the far side, people were standing, waiting and waving.

'That's my Gran. She had cancer and died recently.

Even my mum cried,' Melanie said. 'I don't know who the others are, but they seem to know me.' She pointed to a small boy who was waving vigorously. 'Who's he?'

'Your backpack is no longer required. Leave it, and only take your Bag of Rewards,' the angel said.

Melanie placed her backpack next to another waiting angel, and clutching her Bag of Rewards, she turned to Jed, and smiling nervously, stepped through the massive gates. 'Here goes.' She approached the pool.

'Enter the waters of cleansing,' the angel said.

Melanie started to walk down the steps into the pool. She kept going until she disappeared completely under the water.

'She'll drown.' Jed grabbed the angel's arm.

'Watch.' The angel's voice and face were serene.

Jed gasped as Melanie's head appeared as she climbed up the steps on the far side of the pool. Her worn travel clothes were gone, and she was now wearing an exquisite, perfectly fitting purple suit made of a material that seemed to shimmer. Around the collar and cuffs, there were tiny jewels held in place with gold thread. Her hair was clean, and her face shone. She turned to Jed and waved. All the weariness of the journey replaced by a look of joy.

Before she could be united with the waiting group, an angel led her to a brazier, burning brightly. She opened her Bag of Rewards and tipped the contents into the fire. The flames jumped up burning the straw, wood and stones that fell out of her bag.

'What's happening?' Jed asked.

'Melanie is gaining her rewards. Watch,' Sahila said.

The angel took an enormous pair of tongs, and lifted many precious stones from the fire, and placed them on a tray to cool.

'They'll be added to her crown,' Sahila smiled with great tenderness.

Melanie ran and hugged her grandmother who seemed to introduce her to the others who had been waiting. She knelt down to embrace the little boy. 'My brother,' she called to Jed. 'Mum had a miscarriage, apparently.'

The others watched her, laughing and loving her joy.

One by one the rest of the group were called forward to walk through the pool of cleansing, earn their rewards, and be united with their family and friends.

Finally, Jed stood alone. 'I hope I can enter too,' he said, laughing nervously, to the angel who gazed down at him with a gracious expression.

Yeshua appeared, smiling at Jed.

'You now have a choice to make. You too can enter my heavenly country. The pool of cleansing is here, and your family is waiting.' He pointed to the people waiting on the far side of the pool. Jed saw granddad, and his heart burned with joy. 'Or you can return for one year to the dark world.'

Jed took a deep breath. 'What? I don't know. Everything within in me wants to enter the City. I'm longing to be with granddad, and the others.' His eyes looked with desire forward into the place he knew would be his eternal home, and then he turned around, and looked back the way they had walked.

He took a deep breath. 'I'm not sure. I left everything so wrong with mum and my family when we had the accident.'

Unconsciously, he wrung his hands together. 'I can't decide.'

Yeshua and the angels stood impassive and unmoving. Finally, Jed stood tall. 'I want to return, please. I want to put right the wrongs and the pain I caused my family.'

'All wrongs will be righted one day.'

'Maybe, but I'd like to go now.'

'One year. That is all. Use it well.'

Mists started to swirl around Jed. Yeshua, the angels, the gates and wall dissolved and disappeared, and all went black.

28 RETURN

Jed lay flat on his back. He felt nothing. He could see nothing. All he could hear was a long, low, continuous bleep. Then he heard his mother's anguished voice, 'Oh, Jed.'

With all that was within him, he reached out to his mother. His silent voice cried out, 'Mum. Don't give up, I'm sorry.'

The continuous bleep suddenly flicked upwards, once, twice, then again and again. A drop of water fell on his face, and he smelt the familiar aroma of his mother's perfume and her breath like the gentlest of breezes brushed his face.

The bleeping that had been hesitant and erratic started to become regular and more rhythmic. Bleep. Bleep. Bleep.

'Jed?' His mother's voice rose, and he could hear expectancy rise with it. 'Jed. Oh Jed.'

Feeling started to return to his body as if the blood had started coursing through his arteries and veins again. His toes and fingertips started to tingle. His left knee twitched.

'Nurse! Doctor! I can't believe it.'

He became aware of tubes up his nose, something hard in his mouth, and tubes running along his arms.

'He's breathing,' an unfamiliar voice said. 'Vital signs are looking good.'

'It's a miracle,' his mother's voice sobbed. 'I thought I'd lost him.'

'Jed,' his grandpa's voice said. 'You're back.' Grandpa gripped Jed's hand tightly.

He was aware of activity all around him, and he tried desperately to open his eyes, but they felt stuck down. With a swish, the tape that held his eyes closed was removed. He blinked and saw his mother, and his grandparents, their faces a mixture of joy and anxiety. He tried to move, but couldn't.

'Don't try to move,' a man's voice said. 'You can't.'

At that moment his eyes closed, and he lost consciousness. When he next woke, it was dark. He tried moving, and discovered that his head could rock from side to side, and the lump in his mouth was gone.

'Hello.' A nurse wearing scrubs peered down at him.

Jed tried to reply, but couldn't. He wiggled his head to show he had heard, and then, as if the slight movement had exhausted him, he fell asleep again.

Each time he awoke, he managed to stay alert for longer. He smiled at his mother, managed to return his grandpa's squeeze on his hand, blinked at his Nan. His first words a few days later were, 'I'm sorry.'

The back of his bed was gradually raised till he was sitting upright. Tubes were removed, and every time another test was done, the verdict was always. 'It's a miracle.'

'We thought we'd lost you. You were so badly injured and burnt,' his mother said. 'You were in a coma, and just as it seemed you had gone, they tried one last time to bring you out, and you started breathing again.' She laughed a carefree sound.

'Even the burns are healing.'

Jed grimaced. 'Those burns are painful. When they change the dressings, it's agony.'

'Everyone says it's a miracle. You may even make a complete recovery, though there is a query about your left hip.'

Jed looked at the traction that still supported his left leg.

'You may always have a limp.'

'Comes from fighting Yeshua.' Jed's voice was still husky.

'What? You must have been dreaming when you were unconscious.'

'Mm. Maybe.'

During the hours alone, especially during the night when he couldn't sleep, he re-lived his journey. The people he'd walked with, but most of all Yeshua. Even when all else started to fade, his face glowed. Yeshua who'd saved him, Yeshua who led him home – to his real home, the City of Light.

29 ONE YEAR LATER

A year later, Jed lay in his bed at home, mulling over all that had happened since he had woken in the hospital. He had made an almost complete recovery, except for his limp. That alone reminded him it hadn't all been a dream.

He recalled that when about a month after waking up, and he was almost ready to be discharged from hospital, his mother came to see him alone one afternoon.

'I need to talk to you,' he said.

His mother raised her eyebrows at him. 'That sounds very serious.'

'It is.' He took a deep breath. 'I'm so sorry; I've been an absolute brat, haven't I? So selfish. I'm ashamed.'

'It's been hard for us all.' His mum smiled at him.

'Yes, but it must have been awful for you. Dad walking out to be with another woman, and then your selfish son being even more of a pain than normal.'

Mum pulled a face and rolled her eyes. 'It wasn't easy.'

'And I made matters worse. I should have supported you and Isla instead of going off the rails big time.'

'It's hard for a son when his dad walks out.'

'Harder still for a wife.' Jed's eyes were hard and angry. 'It was granddad dying that tipped me though.'

His mum laid a hand on his arm. 'That was terrible. You must try to forgive your dad, though. For your sake.'

Jed's smile was gentle as he remembered the chasm. 'I know. I learned that the hard way.' He tapped his hip.

'I don't understand. What happened when you nearly died?'

'It's a long story and bits of it really make little sense, but I'll try to tell you.' He laughed. 'You'll think I'm nuts by the time I'm finished.'

Mum sat back and listened as Jed re-told most of what had happened. Finally, he said, 'I arrived at the gates of the City of Light with the others. They all went in, but Yeshua gave me a choice whether to come back or stay.'

Mum gasped. 'You chose to come back.'

'Yup but …' his voice tailed off. 'Hold tight.' He took another deep breath. 'It's only for a year.'

'Oh Jed.' Mum's eyes filled with tears, and she put a hand to her face. 'Only a year.'

Jed grabbed his mum's hand. 'I'm determined to make it up to you. To be the son I should have been. No more being horrible!'

Mum stood up, and gave him a long hug, and then kissed his cheek hard. 'I'll hold you to that.'

For an entire year, Jed kept his word with only one or two lapses.

Once back at home, he was kind to Isla. He was patient, played with her, and put up with the endless tea parties with her dolls. He did his best to be helpful around the home, and once back at school, he determinedly set about doing his best work, and making up all the ground he had lost. His teachers watched carefully, uncertain whether this change was permanent, or just the result of his accident.

His friends were suspicious of him at first. 'Won't last,' Ali said to Tom.

'Nah. He'll go back to being a being a jerk. It's only the accident.'

Jed persevered, though at times he wanted to grab someone, and shout that he had changed, but gradually his old friends thawed, and they welcomed him back into the group.

One evening, as he was doing homework in his room. His mum stuck her head round the bedroom door. 'I'm impressed. You won't be doing GCSE's and yet you're working as if you are.' Her voice wobbled, and tears filled her eyes.

'Why mummy sad?' Isla asked, coming to give her a hug.

'Nothing, darling.' Mum wiped the tears from her cheeks.

'The one thing I learned on my journey was that the things I do now affect what happens later.' Jed grinned. 'Yeshua rewards our best efforts. He's given me a second chance, even if it is only for a year. I want to make the most of it.'

One of the most enjoyable parts was re-establishing his relationship with his grandparents, his mother's family.

'I don't know what's happened,' his Grandpa said. 'But your near death experience has completely changed you. For the better,' he laughed.

'It's like we've been given a brand-new grandson.' His Nan hugged him and kissed his cheek.

Where before Jed avoided them, considering them

old and out of touch, he now realised he had underestimated them. He found he could chat about almost anything with his Grandpa, except music. Here their tastes diverged too much. He discovered his Nan knew far more about football than he ever appreciated, and he even went to see a musical with them.

'It was amazing,' he said to his mum afterwards. 'I never knew a live show was that fantastic.'

As well, Jed started helping at a nearby club for mentally challenged teenagers, including those with Down's syndrome. Each week he helped, doing activities, taking them on outings and being a friend. He loved it. He really hit it off with one Down's syndrome lad called Sam. Jed discovered they shared the same wacky sense of humour, followed the same football team, and Sam was so accepting of Jed, and he too found Sam to be a great pal.

A year had now passed, and Jed lay alone in bed wondering if he would be given more time, maybe for good behaviour. He was smiling to himself when the air shimmered, a breeze blew the curtains, and Yeshua appeared.

'Your year has passed,' he said. 'It's time to go.'

Jed sat up and nodded. 'I know, but I'm so torn. It's been the best year ever, but the City of Light ...' His eyes shone, remembering the glorious city.

The King held out his hand. 'Come.'

Jed took his hand and felt himself lifted out of his body. Together, they walked away from his bedroom. Jed glanced back and saw his lifeless body lying on the bed. He saw his mother running into the room as if she knew. She collapsed by his lifeless body, and wept bitterly, looking up to the ceiling as if for a last glimpse of her son.

Taking a deep breath, Jed set his face forward, and followed the King up the tunnel of light.

30 BACK TO THE CITY GATES

The tunnel ended back at the heavenly gates. The two enormous angelic beings stood; the scrolls unfurled.

'Welcome child of Adonai. Your name is written in the scroll. Enter your rest.'

Jed looked down and saw he was again wearing his travel clothes. He took a few faltering steps through the jewel encrusted gates that towered over him, and shivering slightly, faced the pool. Like Melanie, he put down his backpack and took out his Bag of Rewards. It felt heavy in his hand.

'Enter the waters of cleansing,' one angel said.

Jed tentatively placed one foot, still wearing his thick socks and boots, into the pool. He took one step after another into the water, which was beautifully warm. His body tingled and as his head disappeared under the surface, he felt his scalp massaged with the life giving water that cleansed and refreshed him.

He found he could see the steps on the far side, and as he climbed them he realised that he too was no longer wearing his filthy travel clothes and boots, but a magnificent dark blue suit, made of the most amazing soft material that hugged his body. The suit was trimmed in red and purple with gold thread running through it, and his initials were embroidered in silver on the front. His footwear had changed from hiking books to soft yet sturdy shoes that fitted his feet as if hand made for him.

Despite the water, everything was dry including the Bag of Rewards that he was clutching in his hands.

Another angel stood waiting. 'Welcome, child of the King. Come receive your reward.'

The angel led Jed to the brazier. 'Tip it all out into the fire.'

Jed opened his bag for the first time and tipped the contents into the flames. It too was full of sticks, hay and straw which were quickly burnt up, but the stones that remained shimmered in the blaze.

An angel appeared carrying tongs and lifted out the stones one by one. They had been transformed into jewels – emeralds, rubies, diamonds, sapphires and many others sparkling in the light.

'These are your reward. They will be placed upon your crown, the crown of life you will be given.'

The angel pointed to the group of people, including

Melanie and the rest of his travelling companions, who stood waiting for him. They stepped back as his grandfather rushed to embrace him. Jed had never felt so alive, loved and accepted. Grandad introduced him to the other members of his family. He found he had a far larger number of relatives than he had realised.

One handsome man with sparkling eyes took him aside. 'I am so sorry for all that my grandson, your father, has done,' he said. 'We are praying for him to come to his senses, and return to both the King and his family.'

Jed nodded. 'He caused me so much pain, but I'm healed now. Yeshua restored me.' His hand went to his hip, and a big grin broke out. 'My hip is healed.'

'Of course,' his great grandfather said. 'Pain and hurt have no place here. Yeshua paid for it all on the cross.'

His family led him to a pavilion where everyone sat around eating, drinking and sharing stories of the Way.

His fellow travellers welcomed him full of smiles and loving hugs. Jed was delighted to be reunited with them all, and especially with Jan who was now looking young and radiant. Olive introduced him to her husband and sister who hugged him as if they had known him all his life. He looked at them with a questioning look.

They smiled. 'No regrets. How can we have sorrow when we are with Yeshua here in the City of Light?'

Jed had no idea how long they stayed enjoying the sweetest of fellowship until Yeshua joined them and their joy was complete. Somehow, he managed to greet, embrace, laugh, eat and drink with them all. Everyone was bathed in his love and acceptance.

Jed turned to his Granddad. 'It really is perfect, but I'm so glad I went back for that year.'

Granddad hugged him. 'I know, son. Good call.'

Jed stood up and wandered outside. Everything was alive. Even the air seemed to dance in delight. Jed's face was alight and his heart full. The source of his joy, Yeshua appeared at his side.

'Words fail me. I can't express it.'

'What?' Yeshua's smile embraced him, and his arm draped around Jed's shoulders and drew him tight.

'Everything. It's incredible.'

'Speak to me without words. Show me what you feel.'

Jed's mouth closed and his mind opened. Every emotion of wonder, joy, fulfilment and thankfulness flowed from him to Yeshua, his King. In return, Jed received the affirmation and love that his lonely, battered heart had been searching for.

He was complete. He was home.

Reading this book may have filled you with many questions.

It may have challenged how you think about life or the Christian faith.

The most important questions you may like to think about are:

Where is your life going?

Have you crossed the chasm by way of the cross?

Is Yeshua, Jesus, your Lord and Saviour?

Are you going to the City of Light, heaven, one day?

The invitation to all of those questions is simply answered by praying this prayer:

Lord God, Jesus, I acknowledge that my sins have separated me from you. I am sorry for them; I turn from them and I ask your   forgiveness.

Thank you that you sent you Son, Jesus Christ, to die for me on the cross of Calvary, so that I may be forgiven. Jesus. Thank you for dying for me, in my place.

I receive you as my Saviour and Lord. I give my life now and I ask you to come and dwell in me.

Keep me faithful to you all the days of my life. Amen.

If you have prayed that prayer, tell someone you trust, a Christian friend, or at church where the Bible is believed.

City of Light Bible verses

Nick North: Cross Wires

The third book in the series. Nick and Ashley find themselves in Nazi Germany in the Second World War where tragic events and heroism start a trail of animosity entangling Nick and his adversary, Alex Jenkins, but can they unravel terrible injustices to free themselves from the past?

Nick North: Into Africa

Nick has a terrible dream of a slave being beaten to death, hundreds of years ago. Two weeks later, whilst on holiday in Cape Town, South Africa, he visits a wine estate, the place where he saw the slave being murdered. The Shepherd calls him to right this terrible wrong and to cleanse the land of his bloodshed. Nick becomes immersed in an exciting adventure to unravel the tragic injustice of generations of one slave family.

Katya's Story

Far from home and estranged from everything familiar, Katya, a teenage Romanian orphan, longs for a family of her own but when Maria, a sophisticated Romanian businesswoman, promises Katya a new life as an au pair in London, all does not work out as planned.

Katya finds herself not working as an au pair but instead becomes a domestic slave, imprisoned till

Simon enters her life.

Can he save her from her abusive life? Will Katya ever find the family she longs for?

This is a gripping read on a relevant subject. It's a moving and engaging story about a vulnerable Romanian girl and the challenges she faces.

Great novel reflecting well the real world.

ABOUT THE AUTHOR

Silver surfer, Christine Ottaway, though older in years, loves to write Middle Grade adventure stories, most of which have Christian themes.

She has been an avid reader from an early age and has never lost her love of children's fiction.

After retirement, she was able to fulfil a lifetime's ambition to write Christian adventure stories for readers aged 11 – 13. The four books in the Nick North series are the result. Katya's Story was a departure from this but reflects her concern for young people caught up in human trafficking.

Christine loves to travel, both at home and abroad, and is a trustee at The King's School and is a helper with the youth at her local church.

Printed in Great Britain
by Amazon